THE HOMELESS ENTREPRENEUR

By

Becky Blanton

Dedicated to:

To my late and much loved best friend, June Donahoo, who, when I called and told her there was nothing left to live for said, "Well you know Tim Russert is talking about you on CSPAN. I think you need to leave that pity party you've got going on and start worrying about who is going to play you in the movie."

Cover and layout design by: Becky Blanton

ISBN-10: 0-9970895-1-2
ISBN-13: 978-0-9970895-1-6

Abraham Lincoln once said if he was given three hours to chop down a tree, he'd spend the first two hours sharpening his axe. This book was written to help you "sharpen your axe." It's about getting your mental, emotional and social awareness in place before starting your business. Why? Because when you're homeless you're most often at rock bottom. Everything that can go wrong in your life, has gone wrong.

Chances are, you're hurting, vulnerable, scared, angry and depressed. Life has dropkicked you through the end zone and it often feels like no one cares. You may feel like you're never going to get through it. The longer you're homeless, the more those feelings persist. People around you who have homes don't really understand what you're going through unless they've been homeless themselves.

They're too optimistic, cheerful and often sound patronizing. I get it. I was homeless, not once, but several times in my life, usually by choice, but often by circumstance. What I learned each time was that attitude and persistence will bring you out of your situation. And that's all it is — a situation. Homeless is not who you are, it's where you are. This book is about how you, as a homeless person, an almost homeless person, someone who is broke, poor or struggling, and man, woman, teenager or senior citizen, can change your situation and your situation. You change things by starting where it counts most, by sharpening your "axe." Your axe is your thoughts, social skills, attitude and vision. You can do this. I have. Millions have. You can too. Tell yourself this everyday, "I can do this," and you will.

ABOUT THIS BOOK
What This Book is About

ABOUT THE AUTHOR
Who I Am and Why I Wrote this Book

CHAPTER ONE
Homeless Doesn't Mean Helpless

CHAPTER TWO
Ten Things You Need to Know
Before Starting a Business

CHAPTER THREE
Inventory Your Resources: You're Richer than You Think

CHAPTER FOUR
Businesses You Can Start for Under $50

Chapter Five

How to Start a Business:
10 Steps to Starting Your Business

Chapter Six

Finances: Raising, Saving, Investing and
Managing Your Money

Chapter Seven

Boundaries: What They Are, Why You Need Them

Chapter Eight

Homeless Hacks: Where to Find and Utilize
Resources, Networking and Agency Assistance
to Start Your Business

Chapter Nine

How and Where to Find Resources
If You're Homeless, Poor, Broke or Hungry

ACKNOWLEDGEMENTS

No one accomplishes anything by themselves, especially writing a book. I've wanted to write this book since I first started my freelance writing, consulting and coaching business, but never seemed to be able to find the time.

However, in the Fall of 2015 I signed up for, and was selected to attend, the Community Investment Collaborative (CIC or cicville.org) in Charlottesville, VA.

Over a period of 18 weeks, CIC takes would-be entrepreneurs and start-up businesses through the basic steps for launching a business. Attendees of all ages, from 18 to 70, learn how to write a business plan, find financing, create cash flow and other financial sheets, and market, brand and sell their business idea. They also learn how to give a "pitch" to potential investors and are mentored at every step along the way.

My idea was to start a magazine (*The Virginia Entrepreneur*) for small businesses and entrepreneurs. Even before I knew CIC existed, I wanted to provide really small businesses and entrepreneurs with the information, resources, and connections that would help them further refine, develop and grow their business. After CIC, I was even more inspired. CIC and their mission and students fit my vision like they were born for each other.

Then, while taking the class, I learned several of my classmates were either currently homeless, or had been homeless shortly before taking the course. Around that time I also met Shaun A. Jones, a Navy veteran and small business owner. Shaun was living in his car, but he had obtained his LLC, and started a house painting business. He kept his expenses and overhead low until he could ensure his business was doing well enough that he could afford an apartment. The awareness that homeless people weren't letting circumstances determine their future sparked the fire inside me that drove me to write this book. I literally got out of bed at 3 a.m. and started writing it.

Other people I've met over the years, including graphic artists, writers, and even a doctor and an attorney who were homeless and running businesses also inspired me.

CIC was launched in 2012, so I was fortunate to get in while they were still young and there wasn't a lot of competition for a seat!

The concept for CIC initially grew from the personal experience of Toan Nguyen, owner of C'Ville Coffee in Charlottesville, Virginia. After numerous conversations, a workgroup of 48 people with nonprofit, business and education backgrounds came together to understand better the financing difficulties faced by micro-enterprises in the region.

CIC took their direction from the Workshop in Business Opportunities (WIBO), a private non-profit organization that is committed to assisting men and women with the drive to become successful entrepreneurs. Founded in 1966 in Harlem, WIBO's mission is to enable small business owners and budding entrepreneurs from underserved communities to obtain financial success by starting, operating, and building successful businesses. These businesses then develop economic power, provide jobs and improve communities.

Like WIBO had discovered in New York, CIC learned that small businesses in Virginia also lacked access to appropriate financial solutions and the comprehensive support system necessary for commercial success. So, Nguyen and his workgroup created CIC and also decided the organization would not only offer financing but also education, mentoring, and networking opportunities. CIC now fosters entrepreneurial success through training, next-level growth, and community networking, among other things.

I especially want to thank David Durovy, my CIC instructor, for his consistent and helpful support. I also want to thank Shannon Beach, Program Coordinator for CIC Fluvanna for being so supportive and encouraging during the 18 weeks of the program. Thank you Steven Davis, President of CIC; and Keir Zander, Program Director, and the entire CIC staff for all your passion and efforts in supporting everyone who has passed through the CIC program.

To the men and women I met while homeless, and to all those I'll never meet — I hope you find this book and a way off the streets. You don't have to settle for minimum wage jobs and life in a shelter. You can carve out a world for yourself. Millions have. Hope always finds a way. Just follow it and you'll see.

ABOUT THIS BOOK

The Homeless Entrepreneur is a business book for anyone who is thinking about starting a business, whether they're homeless or not, or poor or not. It's a fast course in how to start a business that makes you money quickly, cheaply and efficiently. You may or may not get freaking, filthy rich by reading and following the suggestions in this book. However, I guarantee you can make enough money to reach the goals you've set for yourself, and to get off of the streets, if you're persistent in your pursuits.

Not convinced? Consider Colonel Harlan Sanders, inventor of the world's most famous chicken — Kentucky Fried Chicken, better known today as "KFC." Not only was Sanders 65 years old before he became a success, he also lived a life of failed business attempts, homelessness and bad luck. But he persisted and finally hit on the secret recipe for success. He's not alone. Dr. Phil McGraw, of the Dr. Phil Show, lived in a car with his father growing up. Now he's a multi-millionaire.

Suze Orman, lived in a van and waitressed for a living for two months, was taken advantage of by an investor who lost all her money and yet she still managed to figure out this whole business thing. Oprah Winfrey sure wasn't born into money. Yet, she's considered the richest businesswoman in America.

The list goes on, Black, White, Asian, Indian or Native American. The only color that matters in business is green.

Skill and talent don't matter as much as persistence and perseverance. There are children, kids under the age of 10, who have figured out how to buy cheap and sell higher, and who have become millionaires before they hit puberty. If they can do it, you can too.

The Internet is full of free guides on how to start almost any business you can imagine, and some you had no idea existed. Those, plus local resources in your city and state, will help fill in the gaps not covered here. There are just too many variables to include everything about starting a business in one book, so I stuck with the things you'll need to create a foundation you can build on as your business grows. What you will have a harder time finding on the Internet is the fact that creativity, personality, risk and a little bit of crazy belief in your success plays a huge role in becoming a success. That's a bit of what I want to tell you here.

Also, unlike most business books, this one also includes tips and information on coping with the challenges you'll face if you're poor, homeless, underemployed or unemployed. It's about how to deal with the unique challenges you, as a homeless entrepreneur, may face.

Some of you have no car; some of you have an older car. Some are dependent entirely upon public transportation. Some readers live with family and friends, while others sleep on park benches, in shelters or abandoned buildings. Some of you, in essence, are "more homeless" than others. Some of you may not be homeless, but are close enough to homelessness that you can see it from where you are. Some of you are housed, well off and reading this to see if it's worth giving to a homeless person. God bless you. I hope you find it is worthy.

You may be on a fixed income or no income. You may be a teenager or a senior who just wants to be more independent. No matter what your situation is, I wrote this book to tell you that you can start and succeed at a business. You may have to start out part-time. You may fail the first, second or third time and have to start over. That's okay. Many others have done that and gone on to succeed and you can too.

Please remember this: The goal of any business is to make money. It has to be your objective if you want to stay in business. Even the IRS considers your business a hobby if it's not making money after three years in operation. Unless you understand how to create a product or service someone wants to buy, and unless you know how to figure out whether a product or service is a viable option to pursue, you won't and can't make money. To start and run a successful business you need to know how to calculate the costs of producing, marketing and selling your product or service, and then you need to determine if you can do that cheaply enough to make a profit. Then you just need to go out and do exactly that — sell something. Then do it again and again.

You may be a college student barely getting by on student loans and your part-time, minimum-wage job. You may be a single parent, employed full-time, but wanting to make a few dollars to carry you through the end of the month. You may be on a fixed income and need to find a way to make another $50, $100 or $500 a month to pay your bills. You may be a kid or teenager curious about how to start a business with the few bucks you have. Whoever you are, if you have ever dreamed of starting a business with little or no money, this book is for you.

But here's the thing: Just reading this book is NOT going to make you money. You have to go out and put the lessons into practice. It won't be easy, but it'll be easier than being poor, broke and homeless. You have to work it, to persist in it, and you have to believe in yourself. If you do those things, you will succeed. If you don't, you will fail. It's that simple. Millions of people have succeeded and just as many have failed. I mention the stories of immigrants who came to America with $4 in their pocket and built up tremendous businesses in only a matter of a few years. The rags-to-riches stories abound — and many of them begin with a person being broke and homeless.

So, all the fundamental tools you need to have to know how to start a business are here. It's up to you to decide if you are willing to step out and act on what you learn here. I hope you do. When you do, or as you struggle, email me at Becky@TheHomelessEntrepreneur.com and share your story, and pictures if you have them, with me. I'll share them with the world and hopefully we'll get you more business. God bless and go get 'em!

If you love this book and want to buy it in bulk, contact me the same address:

Becky@TheHomelessEntrepreneur.com.

ABOUT THE AUTHOR

"Hope always finds a way."
~ Becky Blanton, TED Global 2009

In 2006, I was homeless and living in a Wal-Mart parking lot in a 1975 Chevy van with my Rottweiler and my cat. Only three years later, in 2009, I was speaking at Oxford College in England at a TED Global conference and an audience of politicians, billionaires, millionaires, doctors, ambassadors and celebrities. I was there courtesy of Dan Pink, former head speechwriter for former vice-president Al Gore, and Seth Godin, best-selling author, businessman and the world's number one business blogger. Life can change in an instant. It did for me; it can for you. In between 2006 and 2010 I was homeless for a total of about 18 months.

Even while I was curled up in the van thinking about suicide, Tim Russert was appearing (unbeknownst to me at the time) on C-Span, talking about his new book, Wisdom of Our Fathers: Lessons and Letters From Daughters and Sons, and about me. Before I became homeless I had submitted a 1,000-word essay to a competition he held. Out of the 60,000 entries he received in 2005, mine was one of a handful selected for the book. In between the time the essay was chosen and the book was published, I became homeless. The book was published six months after I began living in my van. It would, oddly enough, be the thing that got me off of the streets — not because it made me famous, but because when it finally appeared in book stores I would realize I was a writer —and recognize that where I was (living in my van), was not who I was.

I worked 95 percent of the time, but minimum wage and a poor credit score due to medical bills kept me from qualifying for apartments I could have afforded. That's the same story I hear from so many homeless. It's a Catch-22: you have to have one thing to get another, but you can't get that second thing until you have the first. I get it. For instance, if you're homeless chances are you don't have a good credit score (or if you do it won't be good for long), and you don't have an income. Without a good credit score or income/job, you're much less likely to be able to find a living wage job. So, you have to have one to get the other. That's part of why it's so hard to get off the streets, or out of poverty. It's like you continue to be punished for your choices or misfortune.

Fast forward to 2015. I'm now a ghostwriter for Fortune 500 Company CEOs and am the publisher of a new magazine for small business entrepreneurs called, *The Virginia Entrepreneur.* I'm an associate editor for *Airstream Life Magazine* and a published author. Not bad. I'm not rich, but I have my own small business, and I'm not living in my van unless I choose to while I travel. If I can do it, you can do it. I'm 60 years old, so don't say you're too old. I also have health issues, including chronic fatigue, diabetes, and fibromyalgia, but I've found ways to work around those. You can too.

Before I became homeless, I was a journalist, photographer, and avid camper. I was used to living in RVs, campers, cars and tents. What I wasn't used to was being treated like and called "homeless." I wasn't used to having severely limited choices — something being homeless does to you.

Becoming homeless was a massive culture shock, physical shock and most of all an emotional shock. I don't advocate it for anyone. If you're one of these people who think "practicing" homelessness or sleeping outside as part of a project to help you understand the homeless has given you a taste of what it means to be homeless, you're wrong. It's not the physical discomfort that makes homelessness so devastating.

It's the emotional shock of knowing you have nowhere to go, no money, no shelter, extremely limited choices and no one helping you get through the day-to-day of finding shelter, safety, food and even a toilet or shower. You can't experience that feeling unless you truly are homeless, just as you can't understand poverty if you have a credit card in your back pocket or family or friends who are willing to bail you out when you get tired of playing poor. That's why this book is doubly important.

Starting a business can do for you what nothing else can — it can give you a sense of worth, purpose and hope. It gives you daily goals to strive for, and something to focus on instead of all you don't have. Doing that is often enough to get you out of the homeless trap. While I've met many homeless people who choose homelessness so they can save money on housing, utilities and bills, they all pay the price in other ways — stress, the stigma of living in their vehicle and of appearing homeless because they're poor, not out of choice.

It's very hard for anyone to find showers, a safe place to sleep and a healthy diet while homeless. Even if you're homeless by choice, you still pay in some way, with your health, attention, focus, etc. If you're currently homeless you know what a struggle it is to stay clean, sleep soundly and manage your life while you try to make a living, get a job or survive. Starting a business, even for one day, like Jim, whose story I tell in Chapter Three, can often get you through the tough times.

This book isn't the end-all, be-all, how-to-be-an-overnight-business-success book. It's not meant to be. That's not why I wrote it. I wrote it because I know there is no silver bullet to success. There is no "get rich quick" solution. There is practical, realistic advice and stories about how others have turned around their lives. It's not magic. It's work. This information and advice in this book are supposed to give you hope and get you going.

Once you do that, you'll learn what else you need to know, and you'll figure out what you need to do to get to where you want to go.

This book may help some of the addicted, the mentally ill and those who are chronically homeless due to severe mental and medical issues, but it's not directed at those. Sadly, there are homeless people on the street who literally cannot fend for themselves and need more robust and supervised programs than a book can provide. If I offer anything, it's this book and a suggestion that those who work with the severely ill or chronically homeless can find some way to create a business that generates income for that population. They may not be able to start their own business, but there's no reason you can't start a business and employ them. There are no magic, one-size fits all solution. There are only people who care, people who are motivated and people who persevere and give back.

CHAPTER ONE
Being Homeless Doesn't Mean You're Helpless

"A castaway in the sea was going down for the third time when he caught sight of a passing ship. Gathering his last ounce of strength, he waved frantically and called for help. Someone on board peered at him scornfully and shouted back, "Get a boat!" ~ Daniel Quinn, Beyond Civilization: Humanity's Next Great Adventure*

Officially, being homeless means you don't have a permanent or government-approved structure in which to live. Unless you work for the government, they don't consider tents, trucks, cars, sheds and transient structures to be acceptable housing. The reason? They can't tax it or you. There's no money in temporary structures for local, state or federal agencies, and so criminalizing or forbidding people to live in their vehicles, or in a tent in someone's yard, forces people to either fly under the radar or ignore the law and suffer the consequences if they're caught. Being homeless is more about being impoverished, poor, having little or no money to your name than it is on where you live.

Being homeless is about being considered a blight on the city or area where you're homeless because you have no money. According to your critics, you're not welcome because you're not contributing to the local economy or tax base. You're obviously and visibly poor. In the land of spend, spend, spend and over-the-top shows of wealth, that kind of sparse lifestyle stands out.

Society, in general, believes that each of us is responsible for finding a way to provide the most basic of services for ourselves, including housing, food and work. Those who don't, can't or won't provide for themselves are seen as lazy, unmotivated, addicts, mentally ill or criminals. This origin of disdain and disrespect for the poor and homeless goes way back, to a time when being poor meant being out of favor with God. If you were wealthy then you had done well and had been blessed by God, and if you were poor you must be involved in some heinous secret sin only God could see, so He pulled His favor from you, resulting in your poverty.

I could fill a chapter with all the messed up ideas people have about poverty and homelessness, but it would only depress you as it did me when I researched it. What I will point out is the fact that millions of people live in very expensive campers, conversion vans or RVs and are rarely harassed or called homeless. In fact, there's a billion-dollar industry that caters to these folks. They're called "full-timers" because they live in RVs "full-time" and travel. Most don't own a home. If they do, they rent it out while they travel. Many are retired and don't work. They fund their lives with part-time jobs, pensions and retirement savings or by working at the campgrounds where they stay year-round. They often sleep in Wal-Mart parking lots or federal campgrounds, or on the streets or in empty parking lots — just like the homeless who live in their cars. So what's the difference? Full-timers have, or appear to have — MONEY. If you don't believe me, look at the multi-million dollar trade shows where these "homes" are sold — often for more than $50,000 or $150,000. They are homes-on-wheels, yet society endorses these people living out of a vehicle, yet criticizes others of us who sleep in our cars. What's the difference?

Wal-Mart loves full-timers staying in their lots because a Wal-Mart study discovered the average RVer spends $151 at their stores when they camp there overnight. Obviously some people just buy cereal and milk, or spend a few gratuitous dollars for the privilege, while others may buy tires and a thousand dollars worth of goods. The bottom line is, campers who stay overnight in Wal-Mart in RVs spend money.

The poor and homeless spend money when they park there overnight too. Why? Because Wal-Mart's prices are lower than most stores, the poor shop there regardless of their housing status. I spent at least $300 a month in the

Highlands Ranch Wal-Mart in Denver, but after all, I was practically living in their parking lot at the time. I parked there at night, went to work in the morning and returned at night. I bought all my food there, a bag or two of ice every few days, dog and cat food, toilet paper, a cot, sleeping bag, everything I needed to outfit my van. If I took up a parking space during their slow times was that any skin off of their nose? No. They were very tolerant of me, and I'm grateful for it.

So, don't buy into society's story that you are a bum, a loser, a thief or unblessed by God because you're homeless! It's not about not having a home. It's about not having money. It's a judgment on a life and a situation people haven't experienced first-hand. It's their problem and will only become yours if you let it.

I recently hired a "homeless" man to paint my office. He wasn't out on the streets wandering around looking for work. He is a businessman who happens to live in his car by choice. The only difference between Shaun A. Jones and any other businessman is Shaun doesn't have a permanent home or apartment. He sleeps in his car. He is a Navy veteran with an honorable discharge. And he owns a house painting business. He has an LLC. His business name is Painters Unlimited, LLC. He pays taxes, sends invoices and does everything any painting business would do. He's also an accomplished body builder and an engineering student at a local community college near here. Opting for sleeping in his car versus spending $1,000 a month for rent and utilities helps him save money. He puts that money back into his business and towards tuition. He has a girlfriend who lives with her parents. She is doing the same thing — working and saving money for school. He sometimes stays at their house when he needs a good meal, a long shower or a good night's sleep. Otherwise, he is a member of a local gym and works out there after a long day painting. However, when I mention that he's homeless people automatically make assumptions about him.

He's one of the inspirations for this book. When I first quit my job, bought a van and started working as a freelance photographer, I too was a "homeless entrepreneur." I didn't consider myself homeless until I was unable to afford an apartment when I wanted an apartment, and some of my co-workers at Camping World started calling me "that homeless woman."

Because I didn't drive an expensive RV and I was broke ... to them I was part of what people consider the lowest class on earth — the homeless. So, it's not the being without a home that angers people as much as it is about your not having any money, fewer choices and a need for social services. When you're homeless, you get labeled. No matter who you were, how successful you were before, the instant you're homeless people treat you like an outcast. People stop seeing who you are, what your skill sets are, what you were and who you were before being homeless, and who you will be when you get an apartment or home again.

Even the wealthy get the same treatment. After my TED talk, during that same week, a female physician came up to me, wanting to share her story. She, for reasons I forget now, decided to take a year off from her very successful medical practice and live on a boat on one of the canals in the Netherlands.

"You'd have thought," she told me, "that I had suddenly gone mad. People who had been my good friends before now looked at me like I was there to steal their silver." She went on to describe how what she thought was going to be a year of adventure suddenly became a year in which she learned who her real friends were.

Appearances, she concluded, really did mean more to people than who a person truly was. A year or so later she sold her boat, moved back into her home and resumed her medical practice. She said the experience left her a bit jaded, cynical and sad. Seeing first-hand how much value people place on having a traditional home, job and career was an eye-opener for her, as it was for me.

If you had a middle-class job before becoming homeless, I'm sure you're experiencing a similar awakening and culture shock. Being homeless is not at all what you thought it would be; yet here you are. So how did it happen to you?

There are millionaire and billionaire eccentrics — businessmen and women who also don't have a home. They travel the world for business and live in hotels. No one looks sideways at them. Over-the-road truckers live in their very expensive truck cabs, preferring not to pay rent or a mortgage on a place they never stay in.

There are millions of people in different professions that require them to travel. They have discovered it's cheaper to live in their vehicles, to essentially "be homeless" and to save money for their retirement than to make mortgage payments. People don't see or treat them as homeless, even though they technically are because they have a job, a business, a routine, money and appear to be normal. But they do consider them odd and strange.

During the time I was homeless, I worked as a customer service representative at Camping World. However, I wasn't shunned and bullied until co-workers found out I was homeless. Once word got out, then I was ignored, shunned and diminished by most of my co-workers. There were a few people who tried to help, but it wasn't pleasant. One offered to keep my dog for me, then turned her loose. It took me two days of searching and three tanks of gas to finally find her.

Others helped me try to find affordable housing, and one even paid for a week's worth of camping fees at a local campground. Yet, I remember thinking, "We sell stuff to people who live in their vehicles, and yet the attitude of most of the employees about RVers was, "They're weird," but okay.

I lived in my vehicle, yet I was "homeless." It all went back to money. If I'd been living in an RV, or even a new conversion van, I don't think I'd have been treated quite the same. The problem isn't that you don't have a home. It's that you don't have money. People don't care where or how you live as much as they care about how much money you have.

Society uses the fact of where you live and your standard of living to place a value on who you are as a person. The first judgment they make is housing, and then what kind of car you drive, or clothes you wear. Sounding familiar? Yes. It's all about appearances because appearances communicate wealth. It's financial profiling. Money = power, or rather the perception you have money = power. I know dozens of families living paycheck-to-paycheck and even without basic utilities in their McMansions because they believe they could not enjoy the social privileges they do if people didn't think they had money.

Society says you can't enjoy life, travel or start a business or go to school unless you have a traditional house or apartment. But that's a lie. You can do anything you want if you have the desire, drive and money. And that's what homelessness is really about — poverty and being without money.

According to society, if you are homeless, i.e. without a permanent structure approved and designated by the government as a "home" or dwelling, then that's all you are. There is no room in their reality for the fact that you are not what your circumstances are at any given time.

When Hurricane Sandy hit the New Jersey area a few years ago a friend and colleague of mine, author Mike Michalowicz, was hit hard and left without power for weeks. He had a house to sleep in, but he had to walk to a local community center, with his laptop and office supplies in his backpack to keep his business going. It wasn't easy, but he did it. Since then Mike has begun embracing his status of the "backpack CEO," as he calls himself. He has an office but says most of his work is conducted out of his backpack while he's on the move. He pulls out his power strips, laptop, and cell phone anywhere — from a taxi to an airport, or coffee shop and works just fine. The difference between the average homeless person and Mike is, Mike has money. He has an income and a business that lets him choose this mobile lifestyle.

People respect; even envy his way of life. It's not about the housing. It's about financial freedom and choices because you have what so many don't — money.

I know that thousands of people in Alaska live in tents or yurts. Many are government employees working for the parks departments. Their tents are considered "home," yet everyday police around the country tear down and break up similar "tent cities" that house the homeless. Why? Members of the military live in tents, huts, shacks, sheds or foxholes. It's part of their job. Why is it okay for them and not for you or I? Ask Uncle Sam. I'm guessing it all goes back to money — who has it and who doesn't.

What I'm trying to say is that this whole "homeless" issue isn't about housing. It's about money. If you don't have money, and you don't have a home, then people are going to chase you down and force you into a living situation you may or may not want. They do that only because they think you're some kind of blight if you're not paying half of your income in taxes.

Contrary to popular belief, not everyone wants, needs or has to live in a permanent structure. That's the government's idea. Why? Because when you live in a house you pay taxes and ultimately, having money, or the illusion or impression of having it, is what social acceptance is all about.

One of the things I found most hysterical is how people treated me when they thought I was poor and homeless, versus when they suspected I was merely unkempt, wealthy and eccentric. When I would walk into a Panera Bread Cafe without my camera, laptop and assorted tech gear, wearing black jeans and a turtleneck or flannel shirt, I was given the cold shoulder, ignored by staff, treated rudely by patrons and looked at strangely. The dress code for Highlands Ranch, a very wealthy suburb of Denver, was preppy. I wasn't wearing the uniform of the uber rich and snotty.

However, when I walked in wearing the same outfit, but with my camera bag, laptop and assorted electronic gear with me, things were different. I experimented with spreading the electronics and gear out on the table to work with as I ate. I noticed that staff who walked by would ask if I needed anything, and customers would strike up conversations, asking if I worked for one of the local newspapers. I was who I was, but their perception of me changed based on their assessment of my worth. That assessment was based on the expensive equipment I had and displayed. It doesn't get much more shallow than this. It taught me that what my parents and friends had tried to teach me was that "looks matter." They do. It sucks, but appearances, posture and attitude can totally make you successful, or not.

If you've ever wondered why kids (and adults too) prefer to wear or own name brand anything, that's why. Appearances do matter to a lot of people. When you know that, you can use perception to control how people respond to you and your business.

Appearances are why you buy the most expensive and classy business cards you can afford. You buy Moo.com cards, not VistaPrint.com business cards. Compare the two of them side-by-side and you'll see why. It's all about perception.

For instance, when I was in college I was the business manager for a rafting company. The owners of the company were tightwads and never spent a dime they didn't have to, including on the lunches they offered rafters on their tours. You couldn't find a name brand soda, bag of chips or candy bar anywhere on their property or their tours. Everything was generic or store brand.

They wondered why business was slacking off. One day a customer told them flat out, "You look cheap. When you charge high prices for your raft tour and lunch, then serve store brand sodas and generic baloney sandwiches people feel ripped off." It didn't matter that the taste and quality were often the same. It was about brand names that conveyed quality and excellence.

So they started buying Coke and Pepsi brand sodas. They bought Frito-Lay chips, and they ordered box lunches from a popular, well-known name brand sandwich shop. Even their paddles and gear were gradually replaced until it was obvious that they only used the best brand name equipment and food for their customers. Business improved and they were able to raise their rates. Appearances matter, not because one brand is actually better than another — often it's not. But the perception that you care enough to buy and use the very best is something people notice.

That's why if you are living in a non-conventional shelter, it's important that you always maintain the illusion of having money, at least a living wage income. It doesn't matter if you're living in a boat, car, van or RV. Cut your hair; wear clean clothes and good shoes. Shave. Smell good. Shower regularly. Wash your vehicle. Keep your stuff in the trunk or out of sight. Don't look homeless. If that offends you then maybe you shouldn't be reading this book. Those are all things the non-homeless have to do to succeed too.

If you're working in certain industries, the appearance game might not be so important, but as a general rule, be presentable, positive and focused on bettering yourself. Homeless is where you are, not who you are. "Dress for success," is more than some cliché. It's true.

My father, a children's dentist making close to a quarter of a million dollars a year at one time, once stopped in at a Mercedes-Benz dealership on the way home from lunch at Arby's. He had been mowing the yard that morning and was still in his cutoff jeans; grass-stained sneakers, torn white t-shirt and ball cap. He hadn't shaved that morning either. My father wasn't the greatest communicator. He stuttered, stammered and came across as "kind of slow." Every salesman in the dealership except one older man who spoke to him and answered his questions, ignored him. Dad thanked him for his time, went home, showered, shaved and put on a suit and tie, and then went back. Every salesman in the place swarmed to him, but he bought his Mercedes from the man who spoke to him when he was dressed in rags. I heard that story most of my teen years, that "appearances matter," but I didn't believe it. I do now.

Along the way, it's up to you to decide if you want to make things easier on yourself by playing the game of "fitting in," or not. I pick and choose my battles, and I encourage you to do the same. If you're pitching your business to an investor or banker, wear a tie, cut your hair, and look like the kind of person they'd want to do business with. Be prepared for the harsh reality that appearances matter. They shouldn't, but they do. You don't have to go overboard and have an entire wardrobe of Richie Rich clothes. One outfit is enough.

Back to homeless, not helpless. If you have this book, and you are capable of sticking to something for any amount of time, you are not helpless. You have more resources than you realize. I'm going to help you discover those resources and use them to start a business. With time and persistence a business can help you get off of the streets (if that's what you want), or help you fund your transient lifestyle whether you're a full-time RVer, a free spirit, a traveler, a retiree or if you're homeless.

Why start a business rather than get a job? Because a study of current millionaires and their successes showed home businesses create more millionaires than any other single category. Those millionaires have become millionaires because they saw a need and way to fulfill it, and you can too.

If you don't have a vehicle, even if you are staying in a shelter or are on the streets, you can still start a business. You're not destined to a life standing on a corner holding a cardboard sign begging for money. There's so much more to life, and you can have it.

ADVANTAGES TO BEING A HOMELESS ENTREPRENEUR

The great thing about being a homeless entrepreneur is that your overhead is very, very low. Being homeless, or not paying rent on an apartment, gives you the freedom to be flexible, to travel and to invest your earnings back into your business instead of into rent — until you choose to do otherwise. Shaun, the painter, is ensuring that when he graduates from college in a few years he won't have student loans hanging over his head. He's willing to sleep in his car and do without the comforts and convenience of an apartment now, so he can improve his life in the future. He's not alone.

A few years ago while hosting a yard sale, I met a formerly homeless woman. I was telling her about some of the stuff I was selling that I had acquired while I was homeless. As we talked she told me her story. Once homeless herself, she now owns a hair salon. Her story is incredible. She was a battered woman who got fed up with her husband's abuse one day, so she shot him. She was convicted and went to prison for several years. When she got out of prison, she couldn't find a job or an apartment. She went from prison to life on the street. She became homeless, but she didn't become helpless, even though she could have, given her history and where she was in life.

She decided to become a hair stylist. She found a part-time job and started attending beauty school. For two years, she lived on the streets, or couch-surfed with friends, but she stuck with school, graduated, got a job as a stylist, got into housing and worked her way up until she could afford to open her salon. She did it. Arnold Schwarzenegger did it. Oscar winner and actress Halle Berry was homeless in her 20s. Steve Jobs, the founder of Apple Computer, was homeless. Comedian Jim Carrey and his family lived in a VW Camper van when he was a child. Famous television psychiatrist Dr. Phil McGraw was homeless and lived in a car with his father when he was younger. Today Dr. Phil is worth an estimated $280 million. Col. Harlan Sanders, the founder of Kentucky Fried Chicken, was homeless when he started his business. You are not alone!

Thousands of other CEOs, corporate captains and millionaires have done it, and so can you. Business is your ticket out of poverty. Notice I didn't say "out of homelessness." Once you have money you can choose to stay homeless, or not. My goal is to be one of those full-time RVers, living in my vehicle and traveling. What's yours?

If you're homeless now, and you fail with your business, the good news is, you don't have far to fall. You're already homeless and destitute, which is the thing most new business owners fear most, so why not try starting a business? You have nowhere to go but up.

If you are homeless, you don't have a traditional place to call home, or to live; that's all. You are not stupid or lazy or incompetent, even if you feel that way or people accuse you of being a mooch. You are in a bad place; you are not a bad person. Don't let the bastards get you down and tell that you don't deserve better because you made decisions or experienced circumstances that rendered you homeless.

If you think homelessness is the issue, ask yourself why people who are displaced by storms, floods or fires aren't treated the same as people who are homeless because they lost their jobs. It's all about the money. Remember that. Because it's about the money, you can do something about your situation.

You are just as capable of starting and running a small business as anyone else. I can name too many famous people who were homeless before beginning a business and becoming millionaires to believe for an instant that it's not possible. It is. And you can do it too. It's hard, but being a business owner is hard for anyone, no matter where they live. It's hard in the sense that you have to keep showing up and keep working when you don't feel like it, or don't want to work.

Business is simply doing or providing a business or service that other people need or want and finding a way to do that in such a way that you turn a profit doing or providing that product or service. See? Not rocket science, not brain surgery. You are not helpless. You're simply starting from scratch and have a little bit more to overcome than others, but millions of others have done it before you and so can you. You can do it. Never forget that.

THINGS TO REMEMBER:

- Homelessness is not who you are; it's what you're experiencing at this time in your life.

- The only person who can define you and who you are, is you. Other people can try, by calling you names, telling you that you aren't good enough, or that you're useless or worthless, but it's up to you to reject their definition of you and replace it with your own.
- Millions of people have experienced homelessness and have gotten off of the streets and never gone back. Some are now millionaires. Some are still struggling but have homes, jobs and families. Some are middle-class. Some are professionals — doctors, lawyers, artists, plumbers, architects and celebrities or professional athletes.
- Being homeless is nothing to feel ashamed about, although you probably will feel shame, especially if you were a professional or wealthy before something happened to put you on the streets. Maybe you got a divorce, lost a loved one, became clinically depressed, made wrong choices. It happens. It happens to us all. Shame is a painful feeling of humiliation or distress caused by the consciousness of wrong or foolish behavior. That's all. It's not terminal. It is painful. Take a deep breath and let it wash through you. It will pass. Learn and grow from it. Don't self-medicate to escape it.
- You can and will get through this.
- You are smarter and more capable than you're giving yourself credit for.

- People who are not from America, who don't speak the language or know the culture manage to arrive here and start and run successful businesses, so you can too.
- Being homeless simply means you have a lower overhead.
- You can do this. Maybe you will start a business that runs forever, or you start a business long enough to get off of the streets. No matter what, it's a resource you use.
- You are in control of who you are and the decisions you make. If you made bad decisions before, tell yourself you're going to start making better ones now.
- You are the boss of you. Believe that and become the boss you always wanted to have. It's within your grasp.
- Starting a business, getting off of the streets, setting boundaries, changing who you are is 100 percent doable, but it's going to be hard. It's also going to be harder some days than others, but consider the alternative is staying right where you are. Which is worse? What you know and where you are, or the potential of where you could be?

CHAPTER TWO
Five Things You Need to Know
Before Starting a Business

"You shouldn't focus on why you can't do something, which is what most people do. You should focus on why perhaps you can, and be one of the exceptions."
–Steve Case, AOL Co-Founder and CEO

I have a sign over my desk that I read aloud every day. Sometimes I read it every five minutes. It says, "I can do this." When things get overwhelming, or I'm struggling with clients, or finances, or work, I look up at those four words, and I say them out loud, and with confidence. "I can do this." I do this because studies show how we speak to ourselves literally changes us. It alters our DNA. Our cells respond to our attitudes, our words and our actions.

I know "I can do this," whatever "this" is, because I was once homeless for almost 18 months, and I survived it. I also learned from it and conquered a lot of the fears I had about failing or feeling like a failure. As I started writing this book, I remembered that 2006 wasn't the first time I was homeless. After giving up my apartment to take care of my mother, who had had a heart attack, I returned to Virginia unable to find an affordable apartment. I had a job as a magazine writer but ended up sleeping in on a cot I had hidden in the office after everyone else had gone home. I did this for about six weeks until I found an apartment. Everyone thought I was just a dedicated worker, "first one in, last one to leave."

Then, when I started a newspaper in Washington State in 2001, I gave up my apartment so I could invest the money in an office. I slept in my truck, then later on a couch in my office and even later in an RV in a nearby campground. I turned my startup money ($230) into a $15,000 sale of the paper and a $50,000 a year job at the newspaper four months later.

I knew nothing about business when I started the paper, and not much more about business when I left, but I did it.

I did it because I was passionate about what I wanted to do and passionate about making a difference in the community. I was able to do it because I asked for a lot of advice. I had friends and people who believed in me. They weren't best friends or even close friends, but they were there when I needed them. They loaned me cars to drive when my truck's transmission went out, and they bought newspaper ads so I could afford to print the paper. They traded me food for ad space, and they provided me encouragement when I got down.

They invited me over for dinner, they included me in their family events and they embraced and supported what I was doing. They prayed for me, fed me and loved me. I don't think the issue of my living in my office or showering at the local state park with my Rottweiler guarding the bathhouse door ever came up. I knew I was living an unconventional lifestyle, and they did too. But we all knew it was temporary — while I focused on my business.

No one ever told me I was homeless. They knew what I was doing was my choice and that it was necessary for the time. They supported me through it. I was "homeless" then by choice, as many people starting a new business are. The next time I would find myself living in my car, wasn't so much a choice, but a necessity.

However, many people who become homeless don't do so by choice. They're forced into it, for a variety of reasons, most notably because they made bad life decisions, or tough life decisions or circumstances beyond their control happened to them. A fire, natural disaster or health reasons displaced them.

If you're homeless right now, your story is both unique, and not so unique. Maybe you lost a job or were evicted for non-payment of rent. Maybe you got a devastating medical diagnosis and had to choose between medicine and rent.

You might be a victim of domestic violence. Your parents may have kicked you out of your home because you told them you were gay or transgendered. You may be homeless because you're a runaway and needed to get out of an abusive home.

Maybe you lost a child or spouse in an accident, or to a terminal disease, and you're too depressed to function, let alone work. So you stopped working and stopped paying bills and nature ran its course. Now you're on the streets. You may be a former professional athlete with brain damage or an undiagnosed mental illness. Formerly a millionaire celebrity, now you're living under a bridge.

Maybe you gamble, or drink, or do drugs and can't afford to do that and work too. Good reasons, bad reasons, whatever the reason — now you're homeless. Step one is accept it for what it is. Stop blaming, finger-pointing, ranting and raging about it. I'm not "blaming the victim," but I am saying own the part of your actions and decisions that contributed to where you are today. You can't change your life if you don't own your role in it. Accept where you are and turn your energy and attention to changing your circumstances. The more energy you devote to blaming someone, even yourself, or focusing on how your current situation sucks, the less energy you have to spend on starting a business. It doesn't matter whose fault it is, or was. It is what it is.

Study after study shows that those who accept their reality and focus on changing it are more successful and happy than those who do not. Change happens, learn to roll with it. The longer you spend focusing on what you don't have, on what happened, on who hurt you or who betrayed you, or on the injustice of your situation the longer it will take you to change and heal your life and your situation. Set a time limit, one hour, one day or one week. Throw a wild pity party and then move on. Your life is what it is right now and if things are going to change you're the one who is going to have to change them.

There's no need for guilt trips or bashing yourself over the head. Just look at the path that got you to where you are today and say, "Yep, I did that. I made that choice. I should have done this or that, and I didn't. My old employer sucked, betrayed me, had it in for me, did me wrong. I acted that way. I didn't think it through. My _____ (fill in the blank) _____. " Get it all out. Write it down even. Then tuck it away somewhere and forget about it.

The only time regret helps us turn our lives around is when we act on our regrets and change. A lot of times the decisions we made that result in our homelessness seem smart, at the time. I thought choosing to quit my job in 2006, and live in a van and travel the country doing freelance work was a great idea at the time. I still do. And, it would have been a great idea if I'd thought the financial aspect through better.

In retrospect, I can see what I did wrong and how things could have been a thousand times better if I'd done things differently. That's water under the bridge, though. If I hadn't been homeless, I never would have spoken at TED Global in 2009. I wouldn't be where I am today. You can turn even bad times and things into a plus. It's hard to see that when you are in the midst of the bad times, but tell yourself it's going to get better because it will.

The point I'm trying to make is, before you can start a business you have to be real and honest with yourself about where you are and how you got there. You have to acknowledge that you, and only you, are responsible for you and your decisions and choices. Anyone else that comes along, or helps you, is gravy, icing on the cake, an unexpected windfall. What you must acknowledge is that you are not a victim. You are where you are. Blame and complaining won't change it. Action will. You can change your life if you decide to. You are not helpless. You are not hopeless, or stupid, or worthless either. You are you, and that is good enough. Now you need to decide if you want to change your life and make it what you want it to be. If I sound repetitive, and like I'm pounding some sort of drum — I am. It takes hearing this message over and over again to have it sink in.

"You have to agree to change and commit to doing whatever it takes. You have to leave, or set aside, your anger, resentment, blame, or whatever you have that holds you back from succeeding, from getting off of the street, or from doing what you dream of doing."

52

No, it's not easy. It's not easy for anyone. Celebrities, millionaires, athletes and people who seem to "have it all" kill themselves every day because life and what you have to do to survive it isn't easy. Here's a fun fact. Studies have shown that it's not what's going on outside of you that determines your happiness or success. It's what goes on inside of you, inside your head, inside your heart that determines how happy you will be. That's why there are miserable millionaires and happy homeless people. It's what's inside that matters. Remember that.

Change is hard. Being homeless is hard. Being poor is hard. But the good news is, you can change all that as well. Yes, you'll find yourself blaming others, blaming yourself and blaming God and everyone else along the way. Life gets better, but it takes a long, long time for a lot of that anger you're holding onto to go away. But it is possible. It begins with you and your choices.

If what you're doing today isn't moving you towards getting off of the streets and into a car, or camper, apartment or home tomorrow, then stop doing it. No one wants to hear your complaints, and your anger will only derail any chance you have at starting a business unless you can channel or funnel that anger into action. I'm not saying don't share your story, or think about it. I'm saying don't whine and moan and bitch and blame. There's a difference. One has a purpose and a reason, the other is just venting.

The more you vent, complain and get angry the angrier and more frustrated you'll feel. So why do it?

Let's start from square one — accepting your situation. Admit it to yourself — you're homeless, or poor, or broke, or in-between residences or whatever. That's the fact. How you got there isn't as important at this point as the fact that you are where you are. You can't use a map to reach a destination until you know where you are. Once you know where you are then, you can plot a course and start moving towards your destination.

That's why the five things you need to know before you start a business are:

ONE: You're not stupid, and even if you think you are, that's not an excuse. When I started all of my businesses I could barely write a check correctly, let alone balance my checkbook every month, or pay my taxes. That's why God made people who can do the things you don't yet know how to do.

The second part of this pearl of wisdom is that you and only you are responsible for yourself. Stop the blame game. It's taking up too much space in your brain and your heart and soul.

It's not mommy or daddy's fault, or your spouse, or your crappy ex-boss, your ex-lover, your neighbor or anyone else's fault. They may have contributed to the problem; aggravated it, started it, forced you out, or forced you to make the decisions you did. However, you are the one ultimately responsible for you. People may have impacted you as a child, but if you're an adult, your life is in your hands now. People, including family and friends, may stand around raging, yelling and criticizing you, but your life is your responsibility, and you are the only person you can control.

That means you are the only person with the power to change your life. You not only don't have to change other people, but you also can't change other people. You can't get them to love you, support you, accept you or do what you want them to do. That's not your job any more than it's their job to change you to be who they want you to be.

If you don't believe that, then try to change something about yourself. Stop smoking. Lose weight. Get a job. Give up a bad habit. How easy is that? It's not. Even if you really want to change it's very, very, very hard.

So there's the thing. If you want to change yourself and can't change even though it's your life and your choice, how the heck do you think you can succeed in changing someone else who (1) doesn't want to change and (2) doesn't want someone else telling them they should? Have you ever had someone try to change you? How'd that work out? Not so great, right? So, this is the most important thing you can learn — that you can only change yourself and that you're the only one responsible for your choices. That's a tremendous amount of power to have once you claim it, but you have to believe it is true and believe in yourself. Developing certain skills, like boundaries, will also help.

Chapter Seven is all about boundaries and why they're critical to business success. They're also the key to learning how to say no to bad choices. You'll always be learning boundaries. They're a skill set no one masters quickly. If you weren't raised with boundaries (and most of us weren't), you'll have a harder time learning them as an adult. It's hard, but it is possible. Boundaries ensure you get paid. Boundaries teach people how you expect to be treated, so you aren't abused as an adult or as a businessperson. Without personal boundaries, other people's whims will determine how you run your business. Without boundaries, you won't be able to say "No," to things that are bad for you, or "Yes," to things that are good for you.

For instance, I don't start work on a project until a contract is signed and I have a deposit or payment in full. I just don't. That's one of my boundaries around money, work and clients. I've been burned too many times in the past when I started projects, and then clients changed their minds, or cancelled the project, and I never got paid. I reacted by bitching about clients and how horrible they were. Then I realized I had the power to change that. I just had to set boundaries, get my money upfront, have a signed contract with my boundaries and expectations spelled out and then get them to sign it. If they didn't want to sign it, I walked away.

Being treated with respect meant more than a few dollars. Eventually the clients I began to get were happy to pay up front and sign contracts. Once you teach people how you expect to be treated, you will begin to attract that kind of client because you aren't working with jerks anymore.

I saw that some of my clients would try to guilt me into starting a job without a contract by telling me a sad story. They told me they couldn't afford a deposit at this time, or any one of a hundred reasons. I empathized with them, but I kept strong boundaries too. I learned that if I started a project without a contract or deposit that the project was more likely to fail, and that I was more likely not to get paid. If a person can't afford a deposit now, chances are they can't afford to pay the final bill either.

Contracts set the terms, conditions, and rules that both my client and I will follow to ensure we're working towards the same goal. If my contracts aren't specific enough about dates, delivery times, and goals, then the client is likely to create scope creep. Scope creep means they expect or demand more than they're paying for. Without clear boundaries and a contract, I often ended up working on something the client didn't want or wasn't anticipating because I wasn't clear on what they wanted. So, knowing that you're responsible for you and that you need to create good boundaries for yourself is key to starting your own business.

TWO: Attitude and persistence are more important than skills and talent. If you're reading this and thinking you're not good enough, smart enough, young enough, old enough or talented enough to start a business, you're wrong. There are millions of extremely talented people in the world who aren't doing anything with their talent because they don't have the persistence, discipline, attitude or desire to keep plugging away.

Dan Pink, best-selling author of several books, and the former head speechwriter for former Vice President Al Gore, wrote a book called, *Johnny Bunko, The Last Career Guide You'll Ever Need.* It's one of my all-time favorite business books. I highly recommend it. One of the secrets to success in Johnny Bunko's story is persistence and perseverance. No matter how much talent, creativity or vision you have, without persistence you won't achieve your goals. As far as talent goes, you can be mediocre. You can be average, or slow, or dumb or have no creativity, but if you have perseverance and the ability and discipline to follow through, to show up every day and do what you need to do to get better at what you do, no matter what, you will succeed.

You don't have to be the best, or to be the only one in your field, or to have the most original idea on the block. You just have to be persistent and keep plugging away, even when it seems like all is lost. Being persistent means you show up every day, every time you've told someone you'll be there. If your car breaks down, if you're sick, if you don't want to get out of bed, you still do it. Not many people can do that. The only reason college degrees are so valuable to employers is that they show a boss you can finish something difficult. People want to know they can count on you to do what you say you'll do. That's what attracts customers — your reliability. That doesn't mean life doesn't affect you. Family members die, you're in a car wreck, or something physically keeps you from fulfilling your promise.

Did you ever hear of Cal Ripken, Jr.? Ripken is known for his excellence on the baseball diamond, but even more widely known as the Iron Man of baseball for his attendance record. Yes, his attendance record.

Ripken was one of only eight players in baseball history to record 400 home runs and more than 3,000 hits. That kind of excellence won him two most valuable player awards. He appeared in 19 All-Star Games. A 21-year major league baseball player, Ripken is best known for always showing up. Beginning in May 1982, Ripken played in 2,632 consecutive baseball games. New York Yankees legend Lou Gehrig held the previous record for consecutive games played — 2,130. He's been asked about his secret for always showing up, and he always tells people the same thing, "You know, I just play. I don't just show up for work; I show up to work."

He made himself indispensable. That was his secret. As a rookie minor-league shortstop in 1978, Ripken committed a league-leading 33 errors. So he stayed on the practice field doing all he could do to improve. He didn't just show up, he showed up to work, to improve and to learn. Even though he retired from baseball in 2001, he kept showing up, looking for ways to teach others the lessons he learned. It's not an ability learned overnight. And we all fail and falter as we're learning. But the focus is still to keep striving towards that goal, especially when we want to quit.

Every time I think about giving up I'm reminded of a woman rock climber someone told me about years ago.

She was a professional climber and well known in her sport. One day she set out to scale a pretty tough cliff solo. This was before the Internet, and all the tech advances climbers have today.

So, it was harder than she had expected it to be. She almost gave up several times. Each time she rested, then got back up to climb. She kept going until she finally decided she couldn't go any further. She was tired, exhausted, drenched in sweat and her muscles burned. It would be dark in an hour, and she decided she didn't want to spend the night on the side of the mountain. She got on her emergency radio and called a rescue helicopter to pull her off of the side of the mountain.

The chopper came in, dropped down a rope and a rescue team loaded her into a basket and then into the helicopter. The chopper took off, going straight up the cliffside, and as it did, the woman saw that she had only been 100 yards from the top. If she had just rested and persisted, she would have reached her goal, but she gave up as she closed in on the finish. "Put me back on the mountain!" She screamed to the pilot. "I can make it!" But it was too late. She had worked hard but had failed to persist. This is true in so many instances, for so many people — whether it's a job, school or a relationship. We are too quick to give up, and we usually give up right before we would succeed.

Finishing anything becomes the hardest right before success. If you can grit your teeth and persist, you can finish. I've given up on a lot of things right before the end and regretted it. Back in the 80s I was in the police academy and struggling. A week before graduation I was ready to throw in the towel, to continue my legacy of giving up too soon because I got frustrated and tired. Classmates didn't like me for standing up for things they thought I should look the other way over, and my being a woman wasn't such a great thing either. I think there were only three women in my class at the time.

For weeks, I told myself I didn't care if I graduated or not. Then, for some reason, I thought about how often I had given up in the past. I thought about how I would explain dropping out so close to graduation. I thought about how dropping out would impact my degree process. I thought about having to explain why I dropped out to anyone in the future. I thought about all those things, and somehow I found the strength to finish.

I graduated 7th in my class of 21 students, with a 3.75 GPA. I have never been so proud of anything as I was for graduating from the academy. I had stuck with it and completed it. My best friend at the time told me she was "embarrassed for me," because she wasn't a fan of the police, but I ignored her. I had overcome everyone's opinion of me and found it in myself to finish something that was kicking my butt.

You can do it too, but you have to set your mind to it. You must keep going even when every muscle and nerve in your body and mind is saying, "Quit." Rest if you must, but never give up.

THREE: Write down your goals. No, having them "in your head" isn't enough. You must write them down. Don't type them into a computer. Write them down. Write them on an index card, a piece of paper, a scrap of cardboard, whatever you have handy, but write them down with a pen or pencil and keep them where you can see them every day. Carry them in your pocket. Tape them to your backpack or the back of your cell phone, but read and think about them every day.

Goals aren't wishes or dreams. They are a destination you plan to reach. Goals must be S.M.A.R.T too. S.M.A.R.T meaning they must be Specific, Measurable, Achievable, Results-focused and Time-limited declarations for where you want to go and what you want to do.

For instance, instead of setting a goal of "Get rich!" set a smart goal: "I will make $1,000 this month by selling 72 widgets (or whatever your product is), for $15 each." You've just told your brain what you need to do, and in what time frame you need to do it. When you know you have to sell 72 units of something, you know you need to sell between two and four a day (depends on if you work weekends) to reach your goal. That's Specific and Measurable. At the end of every day, you can look back and see what you have done, and what you need to do to reach your goal. It's Achievable. You know you can sell two units a day. It's Results-focused — you know you have to sell a certain number of units to reach your goal. It's Time-limited. You know you have a month to sell a specific number of widgets. S.M.A.R.T goals help you stay focused, on task and motivated.

FOUR: You are not alone. Thousands, even millions, of people have endured what you have, and worse. They survived and you can too. Whenever you start to think that you're the only one who's slept in a public bathroom, or used the bushes for a toilet, or hasn't eaten for a week because you don't have any money and are too ashamed to beg or panhandle, you are not alone.

You're not the only single parent who has had to hide the fact you're living in your car, so you don't lose your kids. You're not the only one who has gone to bed at night begging God to take you in your sleep. You're not the only one to seriously contemplate suicide, or ask if "all this pain" is worth sticking around for.

You're not alone. You can and will get through whatever you're in right now. Others have and you can too. You just have to decide and put one foot in front of the other and get through one minute, one hour and one day at a time. It sucks, but you can and will survive it. You control what happens to you when you start making decisions for yourself and quit depending on others to run your life for you.

FIVE: Get comfortable with failure, stress, and difficulty. No one, and I mean no one, waltzes into success without trials, failures, stress and frustration. Even people with millions of dollars to invest in a business fail and have really bad days. You will too. This book isn't a magic formula. It's book of basic steps. Every entrepreneur, every business, every person struggles with something, whether it's money, support, work, health or competition. That's just how it is. It gets better as you get better at accepting responsibility, making better choices, improving your skills and applying what you learn to what you're doing. Don't bitch and complain about the tough times. Figure out a way to turn them into money and opportunity.

ADDICTION: If you have a drug or alcohol addiction, work on that first. If you do start and get a business running, chances are it won't last if you are still using. This is not a personal bias. It's fact. The good news is, 75 percent of addicts are more likely to get clean and sober, start businesses, find jobs and recreate their lives once they decide to do so.

Contrary to popular belief, you are more likely to get and stay sober if you do not enter a 12-step program or official treatment program! According to the CleanSlate.org:

"The recovery culture claims that you cannot end your addiction without treatment or 12-step meetings, but the facts show that a higher percentage of people end their dependence without ever getting this kind of "help." Moreover, in raw numbers, most people stop without treatment.

The study looked at 4,422 people fighting addiction. Of those, 3,217 stopped their dependence without treatment, others either didn't succeed in stopping their addiction, or sought out treatment when they couldn't stop.[1]

While there's a lot of hope and good news for addicts, the most likely reality is that if you do start a business, a significant portion of your profits will go towards buying more of your drug of choice and not to furthering your business. Get sober first. The stress of starting a new business (for the majority of us) is too much to handle while you're addicted. If you're newly sober, it's really going to challenge you. It can be done, but not by many. You simply won't have the clarity of mind to make the decisions you need to make if you're high or drunk. You just won't.

---

[1] *Substance Dependence Recovery Rates With and Without Treatment. The Clean Slate. http://www.thecleanslate.org/self-change/substance-dependence-recovery-rates-with-and-without-treatment/*

Addiction experts say that people don't give up their addiction or seek treatment until they lose something very important to them because of their addiction. For some addicts, it's their family or kids. For others, it's the dream of a lifetime. I had lunch with a friend one day who told me about her brilliant but drug-addicted brother. He was a heroin addict and a very talented musician. He was offered an once-in-a-lifetime album contract with Warner Brothers, and then later lost it because of his heroin addiction. It took losing his lifetime dream of being a recording artist with a big studio to convince him to get help.

My uncle, a life-long alcoholic, went cold turkey and gave up his lifelong addiction to alcohol when a nephew was in a serious car accident after spending the night drinking with him. His nephew, with his toddler son, were on their way home when they rear-ended a tractor trailer truck doing 65 miles per hour on a rainy highway. Other people have to lose a loved one in an accident, a divorce or to another lover because of their addiction. As the saying goes, you have to hit bottom, losing or experiencing the worse thing that could happen to you, before you change. It's up to you to decide to change. Nagging friends, relatives or family can't badger you into it.

It has to come from you. I have several alcoholic friends. I love 'em, but I limit my interactions with them because there are just things they're not capable of doing. They aren't always responsible or dependable, both qualities you must have to succeed at business. That said,

I'm not going to tell you that you can't run a business if you're an addict. Drug dealers do it all the time. Yes, selling drugs is a business, although it's an illegal one and one that I don't support. I know that if you want something badly enough, even if you are an addict, you'll find a way to make it happen. The best and most successful drug dealers, by the way, don't use their products. They know that addiction will destroy their business. They're not stupid. And, you shouldn't be either. Starting your own business and getting sober can work, or it can push you into using more. Only you know what you're willing to do to start a business or get sober. Use the principles in this book, but find some experts, a support group or some kind of friend, counselor or reason to help you get clean. A business can be the focus and can become your new, healthy addiction and help you get clean and sober. It's up to you.

Finally, don't let anyone tell you that you're too old, too young, too stupid, too anything to start a business. Business isn't rocket science. Business is providing a product or service someone wants or needs for a price that allows you to produce the product or service at a profit. If you buy a six-pack of water at Wal-Mart for $2.95 and sell each bottle for $1.50, you just made $9. Subtract your break-even cost of $2.95 and you now have a profit of $6.05. That's business. Scale it, or make it grow, and that $6.05 can turn into $605 or $6,000 or more.

Heck, if you have a package of 20 cigarettes at $6 a pack you've just paid 34 cents per cigarette. If you sell each cigarette for 50 cents, you'll make $3.20 profit. If you sell each cigarette for 75 cents each, you'll make $15, or profit after your $6 investment, of $9. Reselling cigarettes is illegal, but it's a good example. You can resell soda, water and gum, or anything you can buy, find, make or barter for. There are wholesale places where you buy cigarette lighters, sunglasses and all kinds of items cheap, and then resell them to people at a higher price. You can make something or provide a service and do the same. You can also busk (entertain people for donations). That's all business is — providing a product or service for money. Kids with lemonade stands do it. Teens with lawn care businesses do it. You can do it too.

CHAPTER THREE

Inventory Your Resources —
You're Richer Than You Think

"It's not enough to just have potential. You also need to know what to do with it." ~ Susan Gale

Jim — and I call him Jim because I don't remember his name — had nothing but the clothes on his back, a ragged daypack he had lashed an equally ragged sleeping bag to, and a pocketful of change. It was October and Denver, Colorado, was well into winter, with an early snowfall already pushing three foot deep drifts into the corners of the shopping centers.

Like me, Jim had been homeless for quite some time. Also like me, he wanted to get out of Denver and go home, where he had friends and family he could stay with while he got back on his feet. It beat sleeping outside through a brutal Colorado winter.

A bus ticket to Kansas City, Missouri, where he was headed, cost about $140 plus tax. He figured he needed money for food and cigarettes along the way as well since it was a two-day bus ride. Jim only had about $2 to his name. So he did what a lot of homeless people do: he panhandled about $5 in 30 minutes, and then he did something I thought was pretty remarkable.

He thought about how he could turn that $5 into $20, and that $20 into $140. A quick inventory of his pockets and pack and the surrounding area gave him the idea for his business. He needed a product, money and labor to produce the product, a selling price that would net him a profit, and resources to draw upon to create his business:

PROBLEM OR PAIN POINT: It was cold, and when it's cold in Denver, people like to get a fire going in the fireplace. Solution: Firewood and fire starters. The grocery stores sold firewood logs, but not kindling. It was kindling that people really needed to get those logs burning, but there was nowhere nearby that sold kindling. Where was Jim going to find kindling? In the woods next to the Safeway Grocery Store, of course.

PRODUCT TO SELL: Bundled kindling.
Direct Costs: Total cost was $5.45. Wood kindling (Free), Sisal twine $3.50 for a 300-foot roll, and a Sharpie Marker for $2.19 plus sales tax.

BREAK EVEN: Jim didn't whip out a spreadsheet, but he did some quick figuring in his head to figure out his "break-even" costs. Break-even costs are what you need to make to break even, or pay for your goods and/or materials. He would need cord to tie his kindling bundles up with, and he'd need a sign advertising his product. He'd only need to sell one bundle of kindling to recoup or "break even" on his costs (twine and a marker). Anything over that was profit. Jim figured he'd need to sell 15 bundles at $10 each (half of the cost of the wood logs he saw outside the store) to buy his bus ticket at $140. Anything he sold over those 15 bundles would give him the money he needed for food, etc. Now Jim knew what he had to gather and bundle in order to buy his ticket and have enough for food.

So, he bought the twine and marker from Safeway. Then he went into the woods and spent a couple of hours in the early afternoon gathering kindling — which was free — of various sizes and in a large enough quantity that people would be happy to buy the bundles. He created 25 bundles. At $10 each, if he sold them all he'd make $250, enough for a ticket, food and a hotel room once he arrived in Kansas City.

Once he gathered all the wood into small piles, it took him another couple of hours to bundle the kindling and tie it up and haul it back to Safeway where he had already gotten permission to set up "shop" in the parking lot. He got cardboard from the store for free by breaking down a cardboard box the store was going to recycle and he used the Sharpie to write a sign that said "Kindling for sale, $10" and another sign that said, "Homeless, not begging, but trying to earn bus ticket home. Please buy a bundle and help me out."

It was Jim's sign that made me stop and talk to him. He was halfway to his goal when I saw him. At that point it had taken him, he estimated, about six hours to make $60. It was now about 6 p.m. and traffic was picking up at the store and people were stopping to look at his bundles. He sold three bundles in the ten minutes or so I was talking to him, then as I was leaving he sold the remaining bundles to a man who said he hated finding kindling and just bought all of Jim's bundles.

The thing was, several of the people saw Jim's sign and gave him a $20 bill, and said keep the change, or threw in a few extra bucks. One woman bought him a sandwich and cup of hot coffee from the store and brought it out to him. By the time Jim finished helping his last customer he figured he'd made a little over $300, including sales and "donations." A lot of people admire the homeless for "helping themselves" and selling a product rather than just panhandling. So Jim's second sign had done the trick — letting people know he was trying to earn the money to buy his bus ticket home.

Those who stopped to talk to Jim, like me, were impressed with his creativity. He was friendly, helpful and positive — all things every business owner should be. His attitude, customer service and personality helped him sell his wood quickly.

Three hundred plus dollars was quite a return on the $5 or so he initially invested in his impromptu business. It was also a good return on about eight hours work. Final bonus? His last customer also gave him a ride to the bus station. He may have even bought him a ticket and urged him to keep his earnings. I don't know. It wouldn't be unusual though. People like to see initiative and a work ethic. They see a difference between a homeless person panhandling and one bettering themselves and working or making an effort.

Jim's business was a one day investment designed to get him enough money for a bus ticket home, but had he stayed there and kept selling kindling, chances are he could have had a very good business going for himself. He probably could have sold kindling there for a few weeks and made enough money to buy a used car, with which he could have used it to live in, for work and to drive himself back to Kansas.

The whole point of this story is, you're richer than you think. Yes, you can collect cans, metal and recyclables from the trash, but what if you take the money you make doing that and buy one or two trash cans. Then, ask businesses if you can put the containers in their business and collect the cans every other day? As you make more money, buy more containers and create a larger can route for yourself. It's a lot better than scrounging through dumpsters, and you're guaranteed cans every day. You now have a recycling business and a guaranteed source of income. That's just one small example of a business opportunity you seize by taking advantage of the resources around you. If you look closely enough, everything can become a resource and an opportunity.

RESOURCES: What are resources? Resources are anything and everything you have on your person, or that you have access to. This includes material you scrounge, find or collect from your immediate or nearby surroundings. It includes your skill set, knowledge and talent.

For Jim, resources included kindling from a nearby forest. For others, it could be cardboard, cans, bottles, wire, lumber or rocks. Just because you can't think of an immediate use for the item, or because an item appears to have no value, doesn't mean it's not a resource. For Mark Horvath, who was homeless for almost 20 years, one of his resources was his pet iguana. He sold tourists the right to take his photo with the giant reptile on his shoulder. For homeless celebrities, homeless people of Native American lineage and others, your looks, heritage or unique features can be a resource.

Are you in an industrial area? Do you have, or have access to, tools, pallets, nails, screws or wire? Is there a construction site nearby where a foreman, or someone with the power to do so, will give you permission to scavenge the site for materials? Is there a pond, a lake or wooded area nearby? Are there flowers, herbs, rocks, stones or natural items you can collect and use?

What items do you have on your person? What is in your backpack or in your car or current shelter? What can you trade? That's where you start.

There's a great (and true!) story about a young man named Kyle who had a single red paperclip, the kind you could find in any office. Kyle wanted a house and had no money — much like many of you reading this book. He decided to see if he could trade his way to a house, starting with the paperclip. His story is online, on YouTube and on his blog (http://oneredpaperclip.blogspot.com/). The short version is, he did it. He didn't have any awesome copywriting skills. In fact, all he did was post a photo of a red paperclip and this statement:

"This red paperclip is currently sitting on my desk next to my computer. I want to trade this paperclip with you for something bigger or better, maybe a pen, a spoon, or perhaps a boot. If you promise to make the trade I will come and visit you, wherever you are, to trade.

Hope to trade with you soon!
Kyle

PS
I'm going to make a continuous chain of 'up trades' until I get a house. Or an Island. Or a house on an island. You get the idea."

Kyle traded his red paperclip to two girls for a fish-shaped pen. Then he traded the pen for a cabinet doorknob, and the doorknob for a Coleman camp stove and the camp stove for a generator and so on. Eventually, Kyle wound up with his house. It's an amazing story, and I encourage you to read it. Go to his blog, www.theredpaperclip.com for the entire list (and photos) of Kyle's trades. Good things happen if you persist. Resources don't always appear to have value at first glance. But, when you come up with an idea, having a list of resources can either make that idea a reality or knowing your resources can spark a business idea.

Don't forget to list your skill sets as a resource. If you're alive, somewhere along the way you have developed a skill set. You may have a few magic tricks you do well. You may sing, dance or have a gift for speaking. Were you a carpenter, electrician or tradesman before you became homeless? Can you wash, wax and detail a car? Change a tire? Wash windows? List your skills. Write them down so you can look at them and see what potential business you can start with those resources.

If you don't have a vehicle, do you have friends who can give you a ride once in awhile? Do you have a car, a truck a bus pass? Are you good at finding things? Can you design and make a website? Skills, abilities and trades are resources. If you're homeless and have access to a computer, there are all kinds of skills you can learn online, for free. If you're not working, why not learn a new skill?

Most libraries have free access to computers if you don't have a computer, laptop or tablet.

Having friends, or a network of people willing to trade, barter or work with you or help you, are resources. In other words, anything, anyone, any skill you can utilize to start your business is a resource. You may have access to a building, a shed or some other place that people want or need. I know of homeless men and women who hire themselves out as guides to college students, church groups and others who want to photograph, film, help or document homeless conditions in larger cities.

Jim's "business" selling kindling is one anyone with access to kindling, and a community of people with fireplaces, can replicate.

I met an elderly gentleman in a wheelchair sitting at a traffic light at a large intersection near Raleigh, North Carolina, a few years ago. He had a very large umbrella strapped to his chair to protect him from sun or rain. On one side, he had a dog; on the other side he had a very large cooler filled with ice and water. A sign said, "Ice Cold Bottled Water $2."

When you pulled up to the light and motioned for a bottle of water, he would extend a large pole with a large can bolted to it on one end. You put your money in the can. He would carefully pull the pole back in, take the money out and put your change and a bottle of water in the can and hold it back out to you. Many people whom I watched would put a $5 bill in the can, take their water and tell him to "keep the change."

At approximately 25 cents a bottle retail (his cost), this man — let's call him Fred — was making about $1.75 profit per bottle. His nephew dropped him off about 10 a.m. and picked him up around 7 p.m., checking on him periodically throughout the day and bringing him extra water and ice as needed. Fred told me he didn't believe in handouts, and that as long as he could work, he would. He wouldn't tell me how much he made every day, but judging by the traffic and the customers I saw over the course of our talk, I'd say Fred was doing well — at least a couple of hundred dollars a day. It was a major intersection and Fred had two cases of water in his cooler and four to six cases stacked behind his chair under a tablecloth. Fred was not going to starve selling water. Business was very brisk. He said he was only out there a couple of days a week and that people "were good" to him and often gave him tips. I tried to visit Fred again, but I think all my questions spooked him, and he moved to another intersection. I never saw him again.

You don't have to be in a rural area to make money like Fred and Jim. I met an elderly black man in New York City in the 70s when I was living there for the summer. He too had his own business. He collected wire, bottle caps, glass and scrap metal on the street. He crafted the found items into three-dimensional antique cars, mounted on old cigar boxes he got from a tobacco store. He kept his creations in a big wooden box, which he put into a shopping cart along with a small folding table.

He would set his wares out on street corners and sell them for $15 to $50 apiece — which was a lot of money back in the 70s, the equivalent of $25 to $100 today. He wore a top hat and a long black raincoat, a brightly colored scarf and heavy boots. He had a charismatic personality, a deep voice and an otherworldly sense about him. Think of a Hollywood caricature of a Voodoo priest. I'm sure he did well with his business.

I've met or seen homeless men and women make and sell jewelry they've made from nails hammered into crosses. Others have created earrings and bracelets from items they found on the streets or in the trash. Some knit hats. Some make greeting cards from handmade paper they've made from scraps of paper and trash they found on the streets.

Given the choice of paying someone for something they've created or made, versus just handing a panhandler their loose change, I'd say 99 percent of people would rather buy something from you than give you money. They're also more likely to give you more money for something they're buying from you.

You don't have to have a purpose for the items you're listing in your inventory. At this point I just want you to make sure you're aware of all the resources you potentially have at your disposal. Look around. Look down at the street. Look in dumpsters, yards or wherever there are raw materials to be found. Don't judge what you see. Just consider it a potential resource. You never know what might be useful until you know what you want to make.

I once saw a man who made purses and small bags out of the metal discs, or punchouts, he found on construction sites. The construction manager gave him permission to collect them at the end of the day. He used bailing wire and a pair of needle-nose pliers to create a chain-mail effect. It was perfect for steam-punk, and other groups who liked a "heavy metal" (pun intended) look. As a result of his chain mail purses he was eventually commissioned to make chain mail vests and gloves and began to sell them online, making very, very, very good money — in the thousands of dollars — for his creations.

A woman in my neighborhood noticed a feed supply store threw away the burlap bags that smaller feed bags came in. These 100-pound feed sacks were decorated and painted with store logos and other designs. She collected the bags, cut them down, and sewed them into grocery bags, purses, and small coin bags. Her only cost to make them was the thread, zippers, and grommets she used. The store gave her the bags for free. She then sold the bags she made for $40 or more at a local farmer's market. She estimated she made $150 per feed sack after the cost of her supplies.

Pallets, which are free from almost every large store or company, can be broken down. The lumber can be made into shelves, wine racks, dog beds, furniture, bookshelves, book covers, trays and other items. Yes, you'll need a few tools to do this. Start off with a hammer, drill, and saw. Check the Goodwill or a thrift shop or flea market for tools. They don't have to look good; they just have to work. Add additional tools to your collection as you sell more items. You can get everything you need inside a backpack, and even more inside a car trunk or van — including a generator to run your tools. You can also get cordless tools you can charge in a library or other outlet. Keep the tools in your backpack, plugged into a power strip. Plug the power strip into the outlet. Look on Craigslist for used tools. I've seen used tools that sell for $50 to $100 brand-new listed for $10 to $25 on Craigslist. Yes, they worked fine. I know because I own a few of them myself.

Once you start making enough money, rent a small storage shed to hold your tools. Some storage facilities allow you to work (but not live) out of your unit. Turn a 5x10 foot unit that costs $50 a month into a place to safely store furniture you get from dumpsters, the roadside or from people moving out of storage units or apartments. Clean them up and sell them on Craigslist, or through a wood shop or a small business. Maybe you're not handy with power tools or saws and hammers, but anyone can clean up, sand or paint an item. Still not sure how to do that? Search on "how-to" paint, or clean, or refinish furniture on YouTube. I learned how to work on, and even paint, my van watching YouTube videos.

Do you know where you can find a FedEx or copy shop? Many copy shops stay open 24 hours a day. They rent computer space and have Wi-Fi. If your specialty is graphic design, technology, etc. or if you simply want to create a website to sell your wares, you can do so there. Create a blog where you talk about yourself and your business, even your homelessness. Create a PayPal account where people can buy your stuff online. There are hundreds of great ways to let the Internet do your selling for you. It's not easy and will take some work and learning, but the good news is, almost everything you need to know to get started is available free online.

If you can find a 24-hour print shop, work there at night and sleep during the day somewhere. It's safer, and you're less likely to be harassed.

How are your mechanical skills? Some people need bike repairs, and tires changed. There are those who would pay a bike trail mechanic to do those things for them. Have a t-shirt printed up with the services you offer, so you look like a business. Talk to a T-shirt shop, tell them what you're doing, explain your situation and barter your services (cleaning, whatever) for a shirt. If one store says, "Not interested," try another. Don't give up because one or even 50 people say no. Not everyone is a visionary!

If you have skills that you can use to recondition or fix furniture or bikes or fitness equipment, start looking for something to make, fix or sell.

Resources can also include discarded plastic trash bags. Check out YouTube. Some people who use plastic grocery bags and an iron, to make purses, wallets, and bags. Consider YouTube and websites like Instructables as resources too. They can provide ideas for crafts and projects you can do to make money, or start a business.

Even paper can be a resource. Learn some origami skills (YouTube) and sell paper roses, flowers, dinosaurs, horses and swans to restaurants, florists, tourists and others. You never know what will sell, or for how much. If you want to really make good money with paper, learn how to make your own using trash paper. It consists of soaking paper (newspaper, scrap paper, colored paper, craft paper that you can salvage from trash or recycling centers) in water until it breaks down. Pour the sludge (paper and water byproduct) into a screen mold where you can press the water out and flatten the paper. There are hundreds of YouTube videos on making paper. You can either create your own paper cards or sell sheets of the paper to artists (Craigslist, art supply stores etc.).

If you're near a public library, you're near a gold mine. Not only are there hundreds of books on how to make and sell crafts, but nearly twice that number of books on how to start a business. Search the net for ideas for things to make, sell or barter. Take your time. Explore!

Libraries also have tables, Internet, Wi-Fi and librarians who can help you find exactly what you need to start your small business.

When you start moving towards your dream, towards a business, towards getting back into housing if that's your goal, people who want to help you, who can and will help you, will start appearing in your life. Believe it.

CHAPTER FOUR

Businesses You Can Start for Free, or Under $50

"Entrepreneurs are people who are willing to work 80 hours a week for themselves to avoid working 40 hours a week for someone else." ~ Lori Greiner, Sharktank

Remember Kyle? He's the red paperclip guy I just talked about in Chapter Three. Kyle wanted a house too. No, he wasn't homeless, or poor. He did have money to spend thousands of dollars flying around the country swapping stuff that cost $1 for stuff that cost $3 until he got his house. What is so memorable about Kyle's story is that it can be replicated by anyone willing to do what he did — to put himself out there and dream.

What Kyle had most was not his idea or his money. What made his plan work was his perseverance, his sense of humor, a faith in himself and a grand plan. You have those things too. You also already barter and trade. You just aren't thinking big enough. What can you do, what can you trade (including your services, resources, and ideas) for something bigger? How do you take that $5 and make something bigger and better out of it? This isn't a stupid question. In fact, some of the biggest business schools in the country have their students do this same exercise. Why? Because they want them to think outside their comfort zone. They want them to stop thinking about what they can't do, and to start thinking about what they can do! If you can do something with $5, it's easy to do more with $50, or $500 or $5,000.

I know a lot of you are thinking you have no idea how to turn $5 into $50. That's the point. Maybe you don't even have $5 to your name, let alone $50 to start a business. That's okay. You can make or get $5 to $50 pretty quickly if you're motivated. I'll tell you how to do that too. What's more important than the money is your idea for a business. First of all, do you smoke? Do you pay your cell phone bill? Do you put gas in your car? Can you afford a beer or lunch at McDonalds? If you can then you understand the most basic law of all — that you will find a way to get what you really, really want.

It may just be $5 for lunch or a pack of cigarettes. You may find a way to buy a car for $100, and then learn, barter or trade services to get it fixed and running. I have a friend who is an alcoholic. She may let her utilities go for a month, or her rent, but somehow she always manages to find $5 to $15 for the bottle(s) of wine she drinks every night. She's a freelance writer, and tells me she's struggling, but I pointed out that the $500 a month she spends on wine, could launch the new business she's dreaming about, or pay her rent, or her utility bill. I told her she doesn't have to go cold turkey. Just put the money she spends on two bottles of wine towards her business each week. But she has to want the business more than the wine. It's tough. Whether it's wine, gambling, cigarettes or shopping, we all have that one thing we can always find money for when we can't find it for bills, rent or car repairs. Money, and how we manage or mismanage it, is how most of us end up homeless. Learning how to track, manage, invest and spend money wisely is a vital part of starting a business. See how things build on each other? But it starts with the small things — money management and decisions. For instance:

I not only love soda, I'm addicted to it — drinking 2-4 bottles a day (approximately $7.50 a day with sales tax!). I recently took on the same challenge I issued my friend with the wine addiction. Every time I want a soda I put the $1.49 I'd spend on a soda into a jar instead. At the end of the week that money goes into a special savings account.

In time I'll have enough money to buy the camera I want. It's hard, but it can be done IF you want it badly enough. Sometimes I want the soda more than I want the camera, and I buy the soda. It's all about choices. Only you can control you and your actions. You're going to fail. You're human. But don't let that get you down. Get back up and go back to doing the thing you want to do. What do you want more than your addiction or the thing you spend money on now? The decision is yours.

I HAVE A GREAT IDEA —
ISN'T THAT WORTH SOMETHING?

I'm part of a social group online. A new member, a kid in his 20s, started bragging about a "great idea" he had and how he would sell his great idea to any of us for $10,000. We all laughed him off out of the group.

Any successful businessman knows one thing — that ideas, even great ones, are a dime a dozen. It's not the idea that is valuable. It's the ability to implement and sustain the idea that's valuable. If you have a great concept, but you can't make it work, it's worthless. Don't think that the work is over once you have a great idea. This book is jam-packed with ideas, any one of which can make you rich if you implement it and make it work. That's the key — making it work.

I know that you will never get anything you don't want badly enough to work for. If you do want something badly enough, whether it's losing weight, a pack of cigarettes or food, you will find a way to get it if you want it. That's a fact. Even the most destitute junkie on the street manages to find a way to pay for a $300 to $600 a day drug habit. They'll do anything to get what they want. How hard are you willing to work to get what you want? Decide now if you want to start a business badly enough to go after it with the same passion a junkie pursues their fix, an athlete pursues a medal, or someone in entertainment pursues celebrity status.

BUSINESSES YOU CAN START FOR UNDER $50

Here are the typical businesses people start when they have a lot of energy and not much cash. You may or may not find one that appeals to you, but hopefully they'll spark some ideas about what you can do. Let me insert a disclaimer here. In many cities police will arrest you for selling things, or running a business without a license or permit. Yes. They even arrest kids with lemonade stands. Permits and licenses can be free, or run from $5, $10 or $50 dollars and up depending on what you're selling. Check with your local courthouse about what the laws are in your county, city or state. Some businesses don't require any permits or licenses. I go into more detail about that in the following chapters.

SELL OTHER COMPANIES' PRODUCTS: Other company's products include cigarette lighters, bags, clothing and shoes, etc. You buy them wholesale, find them on the street (dumpster diving or curb pickup) and you mark up the cost of the product so you cover your cost and still get a profit. Google "wholesale cigarette lighters" and you'll find several places online where you can buy lighters very cheap — as cheaply as $12.49 for a case of 50 lighters. If you sell each lighter for $1 you'll turn a profit of 75 cents on each lighter, or $37.50 for each pack of 50 lighters you sell. Charge $1.50 per lighter and you'll make $62.50 on each pack. Depending on where you are, and the demand and availability for what you're selling, you can charge even more for your product. This is the old "supply and demand" principle.

For instance, I used to go Crappie fishing way out in the mountains. If you remembered to stop at the bait and tackle shop at the bottom of the mountain, a can of corn or a container of red worms was 69 cents for the corn and $3 for the worms. If you forgot and didn't want to drive the 20 miles back down the road once you got to the lake, there was a teenager at the lake who would sell you the corn for $3 and the worms for $10. Same thing for gas. You could buy gas at the lake for $6 a gallon, or at the bottom of the mountain for $2.49 a gallon. Compared to the drive, the cost of gas and a couple of hours of lost fishing time, those were great prices if you were at the top of the mountain weighing your choices. This teenager was the only supply for miles around and the demand, when it was there, was pretty strong. Smart kid.

The more limited the supply of what you're selling, the greater the demand for the item. The greater the demand, and the more you can sell your items for. For instance, you're more likely to sell umbrellas or rain ponchos on a rainy day than a sunny one.

I know that certain items are in high demand by people — like bookshelves and chests of drawers. I've often made money by going to Goodwill, finding a bookcase, furniture or other item marked down low that I know I can sell for a higher price — like a case of 10 brand-new picture frames I bought for $2 each and sold for $20 each. The television show "American Pickers" is all about two men who turn other people's junk into high-priced treasures by buying cheap and selling high.

You may not have a storefront, but you can still sell items on Craigslist. In my area, someone has started a Facebook page where community members can sell items. It's like an ongoing garage sale. People list clothing, shoes, furniture, tools and even paintings and services. It's free and open to anyone who wants to sell their crafts, tools or whatever they have. Just like Craigslist, you negotiate your price and meeting place where you exchange your items for cash.

SELL BOTTLED WATER AND SODA: Your cost can be as low as $10 plus your permit. You'll need ice, a case or two of water, and a bucket, trashcan or cooler to put your ice and drinks in. You'll need a sign advertising your water and your price. Sell your water where there is a lot of traffic and/or demand, and not much supply nearby. Think busy intersections, parks, and bike paths. Get creative and think about where people might want and need to buy a cold drink. If you have a cooler with wheels (usually about $25 to $50 at Wal-Mart), you can tow your cooler behind you, making you a mobile water vendor. Check with the city for permits you need to do this. You may not sell a lot of ice-cold water the first day, but as people begin to see you there consistently, they will start bringing money and buying from you. You can't just show up when you feel like it because your potential customers will carry their own water.

SELL KINDLING AND/OR FIREWOOD: You'll need access to a forest or land where you can gather the kindling, a permit or permission to gather wood and something to transport the wood in. You'll also need a saw, and a chainsaw or axe if you're going to cut larger logs. You'll need some sort of packaging — shrink-wrap, mover's wrap or sisal twine to bundle your wood with. If you're selling around a holiday season, consider using red twine or string. Make sure the bundle has a handle (use the twine), so it's easy to carry. If it's easy to carry, people may buy two or more bundles. The easier you make it for your customer to buy, the more they'll buy.

SELL YOUR SERVICES: Sell services like lawn care, house sitting, car detailing, sidewalk and driveway snow removal and dog walking. Can you paint? Homeowners always need something painted, stained or cleaned. Electric leaf blowers can be purchased for as little as $5 at Goodwill, or $25 new at big box stores like Wal-Mart. Keep your eyes open at yard sales too.

POOPER SCOOPER: Can you pick up dog poop? Depending on the size of the yard and the number of dogs, lots of people are willing to pay someone $15 to $55 an hour to pick up their yards and dispose of the waste their dogs generate. Hand out or post flyers about your services at local dog parks, or through a vet clinic, pet store or other place dog owners frequent.

Think of services people in your area need that you can perform. In New York City, for a while anyway, homeless people would stand at intersections with a rag and bottle of window cleaner and clean people's windows for a few bucks. Often times they'd just start washing without the driver's permission and then ask for payment, forcing the driver to pay something. If you can find a place to do the same, but with the owner's permission and at their request, then you may have a business.

Window washing, particularly of commercial windows, or even homes is a very good job. It pays well, and you can generate repeat business if you're good.

SELL ITEMS ON CRAIGSLIST: I have a large storage unit. It's in a rural area where, like most storage facilities, people leave furniture, bookshelves, and various items when they move out. They just don't want the hassle or cost of transporting things to the local dump. But storage units aren't the only places to look for discarded, but usable, items. Every month, like clockwork, people move out of apartments, storage facilities and offices. They throw away perfectly good clothing, furniture, and items you can pick up and sell on Craigslist. You'll need someplace to store larger items, but if you have a car, van or truck, you can store the items in or on your vehicle. Check before collecting. Some communities make it illegal to "dumpster dive" or collect items from the curb while other communities love it because it keeps things out of the landfill.

Look for designer-label clothing you can sell in consignment shops. If you're really ambitious, visit apartment managers and offer your removal services for their tenants. Bring a flyer or business cards they can post on bulletin boards. Landlords usually don't want to pay to have furniture hauled away. They are happy to call you when they have items to remove. Even if you sell valuable items for $10 or $20 to move them fast, that's money you didn't have before. If the items are in too poor of condition to resell, recycle them or use them for something else you can create and sell.

SEWING AND KNITTING: Do you knit or sew? Make and sell hats, scarfs, gloves, small pouches or zippered bags and other items. When I was homeless there was a woman making beautiful knit hats that she gave away to other homeless people. That was very generous of her, but if she sold those hand-crafted hats and scarfs for $15 or $20 each she could provide more hats, gloves and scarves for the homeless and have enough cash to get off of the streets herself.

There's a woman in my neighborhood on a fixed income. She just beat cancer last year and is a caregiver for her husband, who suffered a stroke as she was starting chemo treatments. Yeah, some pretty big challenges.

She charges $20 an hour to hem pants, teach sewing, or do various sewing projects. You can too. If you have a sewing machine (or can buy one — they start at $50 and up, and are even cheaper at thrift shops and Goodwill), you can do the same. You can also create small zipper bags and other items to sell at farmer's markets, craft stores and art galleries.

This is another "must have a car" or access to a sewing machine type of job, but I've seen women sewing at picnic tables at campgrounds, taking advantage of fees as low as $5 a day to access a campsite for the day and that includes showers and laundry access. Think about asking to use a community room at a church or community center. Most places will let you use their facilities if you ask and explain what you're doing.

SIGN OR MURAL PAINTER: Are you a good painter? For less than $50 you can start your own sign or mural painting business. The best kinds of signs to paint are more artwork than sign. Look on Pinterest.com for examples of hand painted signs that sell well. If you have an artistic bent, go to Canva.com (free) and make flyers for people who can't make them themselves.

There are dozens of "How-to-start" your own business articles online. All of them begin with applying for a business license and other applicable licenses, such permits for preparing food, selling online products or relevant professional licensing. Some local governments don't require yard sales, or farmer's markets or crafters to have a license. Many people try selling and seeing what kind of success they have, or not, before getting a license. Check to see what the laws are, and then decide if you want to risk being caught or not. I advise buying the permits and licenses and staying legal. But that's not always an option if you need to make money to afford the permits.

These are all great ideas for people who are living in their car, or have access to some kind of storage, but the way this business book differs from most is that I realize if you're homeless, chances are you don't have access to storage or a way to carry inventory or tools around with you. Your primary goals in life are shelter, safety, food and finding a way to get off the street, or get around town. You're struggling to stay warm, or cool, safe, fed and clean.

If you bought this book, chances are you're also willing to work, yet can't find work. You may have a part-time job, but it doesn't pay well. Maybe transportation or full time hours just aren't a possibility for you because of children, transportation or housing. If you're living in a shelter, then you know that homeless shelters are designed to keep you unemployed. Shelters want you in line to get a bed for the night by 3, 4 or 5 o'clock, and most jobs require you to work until 5 p.m. Having a part-time job or being self-employed is the better way to go. You can keep your shelter housing and make money too.

If you are at all competent on a computer, it is possible to make money online, or as a mystery shopper, or through freelance sites like ODesk, Upwork, and others. FedEx or your local library becomes your office if you have a laptop. If you don't have a laptop or computer access, get a tablet with Wi-Fi access. Every McDonalds in the country has free Wi-Fi. Look clean and employed and have a laptop and not many places will question the fact you're sitting in their lobby and using their Wi-Fi. Try to buy at least a drink or something from the business in exchange for the Wi-Fi, even if they don't charge. They're in business too.

ONLINE WORK SITES: There are very few legitimate websites that charge a fee to help you find work. Many sites offer you work if you pay $29.95 or some such outrageous fee to join. Don't do it. There are too many legitimate sites that offer work opportunities and jobs for free. Never pay someone to find you work. The one possible exception is Flexjobs.com. They charge a monthly fee of $14.95 and screen all their job offerings to ensure the jobs are legitimate and not work-at-home scams. Forbes Magazine has checked them out and often refers readers to their site for part-time and commuter jobs.

Sites like Upwork and others offer you free memberships, but may offer you a month-to-month upgrade for the privilege to bid on more jobs. That's legit.

If you are going to pay a membership site for access, use a prepaid debit card, or PayPal, so the company doesn't keep charging your credit card, and so you can contest unapproved charges if they do charge you without your permission. Some of these online job/work sites are evil and will continue to charge your card even after you've told them to stop, and after they've run up huge overdrafts at your bank. If they don't take a prepaid debit card, keep looking. And never leave more than one month's fee on your prepaid debit card.

SMARTPHONE APPS: Do you have a smartphone? There are smartphone apps that will pay you for being a mystery shopper. While smartphone apps like those I've listed here won't make you rich, they can make you enough money ($20 to $100) to get you to a point where you can invest in a small business.

INBOX DOLLARS: Use the Inbox Dollars app to take surveys, browse the Internet, and play games in exchange for cash. Once you earn $30, ask to be paid and get a check within two weeks. Earn $5 just for trying it out. Inbox Dollars has paid its users over $30 million.

SURVEYS ON THE GO: Surveys on the Go offers surveys that pay from $0.25 to $5 per survey. Yes, companies are willing to pay you more than a penny for your thoughts. Companies, political campaigns and market research firms buy the survey data. Surveys take just minutes, and you can cash out with PayPal.

BOOKSCOUTER: Do you have time to spend in old bookstores, yard sales or Goodwill? Do you have a smartphone? Then download Bookscouter at Bookscouter.com. Bookscouter is an app for your iPhone or Android smartphone. Scan or enter the ISBN of your book, and the app will find sites looking to buy it. Bookscouter compares prices so you get the best deal. It's a great way to ensure the books you see at yard sales are worth something before you buy them. Yard sales and thrift stores are great places to find books. Scan before you buy.

Once you scan the book, find interested sites and pick a buyer, tell them where to send the payment, and then mail the book with the prepaid shipping label, provided (usually) by the buyer. Amazon.com also buys back books. If you know your books, you can often make a good living buying and reselling them.

TASKRABBIT: "Taskers" use the TaskRabbit app and website to get paid for the things they're good at doing. Get approved to be a Tasker and set your hourly rate — most usually start from $15-to-$30 per hour — to complete jobs like running errands, assembling flat boxed store furniture, gift wrapping, driving, dog walking or organizing. People who need your services will request you through TaskRabbit.

FIELDAGENT and GIGWALK: These two apps pay you to complete small tasks within your community. Some activities include going to a store and taking a picture of a product display, or checking the price of an item, and filling out a short survey after experiencing a new store. Both apps use PayPal to pay users.

REWARDABLE: Rewardable lets you sign up for tasks that take an average person anywhere from 5-15 minutes to complete, and pays up to $20 per task. The tasks range from checking inventory to comparing prices at local stores. When you want to cash out, hit "withdraw" and the money gets transferred to your PayPal account. Another task app like Rewardable is Easyshift.

EASYSHIFT: Easyshift pays you for doing simple tasks at stores near you, like checking prices and store displays. You need to prove yourself on this one. As you complete more assignments, more and more higher-paying tasks become available to you. Get paid within 48 hours too as this app sends your money using PayPal.

WEBSITES FOR MAKING MONEY ONLINE:

Yes, you can make money online. For most people, it takes a year or more, a lot of hard work and a stiff learning curve. However, there are a few legitimate sites where you CAN make good money online. When I quit my job back in 2008, I made my living online writing on Elance.com. Elance is now Upword, but there other sites in addition to Odesk, Upword and Elance.

FIVERR: Fiverr.com is the perfect place to get ideas for products or services to sell. People on Fiverr sell anything and everything (legal of course), starting at $5 for the basic item and more for upsells. To get an idea of what you can sell or offer, spend some time on their website. There's a lot of competition, so you need a great idea and great customer service to rise to the top, but thousands have done so and you can too.

FREELANCE WRITER: Can you write? Draw? Use Photoshop? Consider becoming a freelance writer, photographer or graphics person at your local newspaper. If you can write, then consider writing and self-publishing an eBook/paperback on http://createspace.com. It's free and simple to do. If you have an expertise of any kind, then write about it and sell it. Sell it for $2.99 to $4.99. Createspace will either mail you a check or direct deposit your earnings into your bank account once a month. They do accept prepaid debit cards!

What can you write about? My friend Phil Elmore wrote a book called, "10 Things Your Doctor Won't Tell You about CPAP Machines." Share your knowledge with the world! Createspace even has a free, online book cover creator. The great thing about writing and selling a book is that it's income every month — something called "passive income." You don't have to write every day. Once you write one book, write another. Even if you only sell 1-5 a month, that is still income and you can use it to start a business.

STOCK PHOTOS PHOTOGRAPHER: Do you have a good smartphone, one with a camera? If you can take good photos you can sell them on stock photography sites like Depositphoto.com, iStockphoto.com and others. It takes time and consistent photo quality, but every site walks you through the process for free. Make between $5 and $5,000 a month depending on the number of photos you have and if you understand the kinds of photos buyers are looking for. These sites send you a check or direct deposit money to a debit or bank card every month. Sales must exceed $100 to get a payout, but once you have several hundred or a 1,000 or more photos, the more likely you are to hit that cap each month. There are photographers making $100,000 and more every year on these sites. You can be one of them. If you want to get serious about it, take an online or community college photography course.

VIRTUAL ASSISTANT: Virtual Assistants are exactly like the name implies: they're virtual — online — assistants. No one needs to know you're homeless, or living in your car or a shelter if you don't want them to. Virtual assistants perform a variety of tasks, from answering emails, to answering the phone, or managing calendars for clients. They provide creative, administrative or technical assistance to their clients and make from $10 to $40 an hour depending on what they're doing and who they're doing it for. Membership to VirtualAssistants.com is $49 a year, or $9.99 on a month-to-month basis. This is the oldest, and best, virtual assistant site on the web. Unlike a job site that charges your credit card and claims to find you work, VirtualAssistants.com is a membership site where you go to meet other virtual assistants, to learn about how to become a virtual assistant and to belong to an organization of like-minded entrepreneurs.

CRAIGSLIST JOBS: Maybe you're not the business type, or maybe you just want to make money As Soon As Possible (ASAP). Check out the MISC. jobs on Craigslist. People often post one day jobs, either moving furniture, cleaning out a garage or something that just involves manual labor and pays cash same day. People posting jobs don't always post them in the right category, so look through all the job postings, even ones you think you aren't qualified for. I once looked through the medical jobs and found a one-week gig shredding medical records at a doctor's office. All

I had to do was feed files through a giant paper shredder. It paid $12 an hour, and I just sat in a chair all day. You'd be surprised at the odd jobs and great pay you can find on Craigslist. Just spend time every day looking. I check in several times a day because people post things throughout the day.

PALLETS: One of the great things I found easy to resell were pallets. Pallets are free from many businesses. You'll need a vehicle to transport the pallet and some kind of crowbar to dismantle them, and a place to store the wood until it sells.

If you think pallets are junk, just search for "Pallet projects" on Pinterest.com. People love to build things with pallet wood, but they don't like to go out and get, transport and break up the pallets. They just like the wood. Many are willing to pay for pallet wood that's been broken up and stacked. I charged $2 to $3 a board for a 4- to 6-foot length. I charged more for oak. And, I sold every board I could get my hands on. It took me about 15 minutes to break down a pallet, and I got, on average, 6 to 8 boards per pallet, so I made between $15 to $25 per pallet breaking down two to four pallets an hour.

Not a bad return on my investment of time, gas and labor. What people didn't want for projects, or that was too twisted to use for furniture I cut up into 8-inch lengths and sold it as firewood at 10 to 25 cents a board, depending on if it was pine or oak. Depending on what area you're in, you may get $1 or more per board. I also collected old barn wood and sold that to artists at the local university for $5 a board since they like to make frames with it. Ask before collecting from someone's property.

DECORATIONS: Christmas is wreath time. You don't have to make wreaths out of traditional evergreen wreaths. You can use wire and beer cans (Fraternities might appreciate these). Use found objects, pinecones, or cardboard torn into holly leaf shapes. Make them large for doors and walls, or small for people's lapels and jackets. During the holiday season, you can cut lengths of pallet wood into varying lengths and nail them to a vertical piece of wood to resemble a Christmas tree that people can post in their front yards. Sell bare trees, or paint them in various colors. Cost? Pallets are free. A handsaw is $5 to $20. Nails or screws and a screwdriver/hammer are less than $15.

You can make bookshelves, wine racks, stools and all kinds of things with pallet wood. Get creative. If you're not the creative type, get on the Internet and go to http://Pinterest.com for ideas.

BUSKING: Busking is the timeless art of performing in public for money. Do you sing? Dance? Can you make and create a puppet show with socks and a cardboard box? BuskerCentral.com is a great place to start learning the art of "The build, the show and the hat," or the way to make money performing. Just showing up and playing your guitar won't necessarily ensure you're going to make money. Don't have any musical talent? Learn to make balloon animals, or do origami (the art of turning paper into three-dimensional animals). Charge a dollar, or $5, to turn a $1 bill into a swan, a camel or an alien. Are you a comedian? Grab a stool, a roll of aluminum foil and charge people to make them a personalized "Tin Foil Hat." You'd be surprised how many people will go along with you and pay you to make them laugh. Learn to juggle. It takes about an hour for the average person to learn to juggle three balls. Practice. Put together an act and start performing. Sing, dance, and draw caricatures of people. Write poems. Create a sign that says "Have your photo taken with a rags-to-riches millionaire in the before stage."

For free videos on how to make money as a busker, go to http://www.buskercentral.com/video.php#how2

CELEBRITY HOMELESS MAN/WOMAN: If you're in a tourist town, charge people to have their picture taken with you. The "naked cowboy" is a guy in his underwear and a cowboy hat. He plays his guitar and sings while standing on the medians and crosswalks of NYC. Yes. He's real. Google him.

You don't have to strip to your underwear to be creative or funny. Get some boxes and decorate them to create a robot costume. Wear them and advertise yourself as the homeless robot of Atlanta, or wherever you are.

Dare to do the unexpected. Be funny, talented and creative, and people will reward you for your busking. I have a free eBook on my website with copywriting tips from the homeless. Go download it. I think you'll enjoy it. www.homelessentrepreneur.com. If you want more detailed tips, there's a $2.99 Kindle version on Amazon.com.

The one thing all these businesses have in common is that you probably won't get rich, or even make a great deal of money your first time out. Then again, you may walk away with a fistful of money. You don't know. That's business. You may do well one day, and poorly the next. That's why being persistent is so important. If you don't do well at first, wait around. Things change.

Okay, so I could fill a book with ideas for businesses, but the fact is a successful business depends on who you are, and where you are, and what kind of "pain" people are in where you are. By pain I mean what problems do they have? How much are they willing to pay for a solution to their problem? For instance, in many states there used to be a service called "The meat wagon."

The meat wagon would respond to any dead animal on a road or highway, collect the carcass and haul it off to a dump or kill pit where it was properly disposed of. Many states eliminated this service because of the economy and because it's hard to find people willing to collect and dispose of dead animals all day.

There are services that will respond to a farm or similar area to bury dead horses, cattle and livestock. The pain is, people with large dead animals need to have them buried or removed quickly because letting them rot in place creates disease, attracts vermin and predators and frankly, it stinks — literally — to have dead creatures lying around. You'll need a truck and/or a trailer to pull this off for larger animals, but if you're homeless in a rural area, there's a demand for this.

Farmers who get flat tires on their tractors used to just fix them themselves. Now that the larger machines weigh several tons and tires are often the size of a small car, the pain for farmers is getting a flat tire. They need to have someone come out to the farm to repair or replace the tire. That's the solution for the pain.

If you have a car less than 10 years old, consider becoming an Uber or Lyft driver. Google either name to find out how this ride-sharing business works. The average Uber driver earns between $18 and $35 an hour, but you work your own hours. There are additional costs for insurance, so check it out carefully, but there is money to be made there. Just make sure your insurance company is on board, or that you have additional coverage.

Picking the best business idea for where you are located will be hard. A business idea that works in Denver, Colorado, (firewood for instance) may or may not work in New York City, or it may work better, but the free wood may be harder to find. Rural towns have different needs than big cities. People tend to be self-sufficient and cut their own wood. However, you may find a community of retirees who welcome someone who will cut or deliver wood for them.

Part of creating a successful business is trial and error, as well as knowing who your customers are, how they think and what they need. If one idea doesn't work, tweak it or find a different idea. Most successful businesses don't begin in the form their owners originally envisioned. They morph, change, shift and grow as the owners improve or change them to meet market or consumer demands. So think about people's pain. What business can you start to ease someone's pain?

For instance, families with two working parents and children need day care and baby sitters. That's their pain — they need someone to watch their child while they work. Day Care Centers and babysitters are the solutions to the need or pain of needing someone to watch your child when you can't.

Look around you. What kind of pain/need do people in your area have? Do they need dog walkers? Cat sitters? Lawn care workers? Cheap fast food delivery? Are there a lot of elderly people in your area? Do they need someone to take their trash out? Clean their gutters? Organize their garage? Haul away appliances?

Take your time and really explore what people need to make their lives easier. This may involve sitting in a crowded area or mall and people watching to see what they need.

Someone who noticed that their purse didn't really fit over restaurant chairs and got dirty sitting on the floor invented the purse hook for tables. The purse hook is a hook that allows women (or men) to hang their purse or messenger bag or daypack from any table. The hook fits into a pocket and can hold up to 50 pounds. It's designed in such a way as to counterbalance the weight of the bag.

Not only does it keep your bag off of a dirty restaurant or bar floor, but it also hangs the purse next to you so thieves can't steal it. The pain/need? Someway to keep your purse off of the floor without hanging in on your chair. It can be used for shopping or grocery bags too, so if you're out shopping and want to have lunch you can hang your shopping bags where they'll remain clean, safe and visible to you and away from bag snatchers.

What's the biggest thing pet owners hate to do? Scoop poop of course. If they have a large yard and let their dogs out several times a day as many do, there's a real demand for someone to collect and dispose of dog waste. Many owners will pay well to avoid performing that task themselves. All you need is a hand rake, shovel, and plastic bags and you're in business!

If you're homeless and don't have a car, you'll need to find a service or product that doesn't require having a lot of inventory. Yes, you can make jewelry in small batches and store it in a bag or suitcase that doubles as a display case, but don't forget to take into account that to make good money you'll need to have a way to transport or carry and display your product, as Jim did with his kindling bundles. You'll also need to be able to carry the tools of your trade or your materials too. Shopping carts work well, but why not design (and maybe sell) a table with wheels?

The best way to get around not having a vehicle or storage unit is to start small. As you sell your items put your profits back into your business — either by renting a small storage shed, buying a used car or renting space in an indoor flea market, etc.

The temptation, particularly if you do well and sell a lot of items, is to blow the money on something you've been doing without, whether it's a hotel room for the night, or food, clothing or a nice meal. Don't deny yourself those things, but start saving a percentage of what you earn so you can buy a car — or save for vehicle repairs and insurance, upgrades to your van, or tires or gas, etc. if you have a vehicle.

Open a bank account at Woodforest Bank — located in most Wal-Marts. Not only are they open every day of the week, including evenings, but they also have free checking and are found just about everywhere you'll find a Wal-Mart. Wal-Mart stores are on every bus line and easy to access. I highly recommend Woodforest Bank. If you don't want a bank account, then get a Wal-Mart reloadable debit card. They have the best rates in the business, and you always know where to go to refill the card. NetSpend charges $4-$5 to reload your card. Wal-Mart charges $3.

Here are other tasks and services you can do and charge for:

MECHANIC: Lots of people are looking for good, affordable and honest mechanics to work on their car. You don't need a garage to do basic repairs and maintenance on most cars. If you're one of the few with a mechanical knack, especially for car or small engine repair, you can find good work anywhere. Check with your local community college. They often offer affordable classes in small engine repair and other skills that you can learn quickly.

HOUSE PAINTER: If you have an attention to detail and are good with a paint brush and roller, consider painting houses (interior and exterior).

GARAGE CLEANER: Speaking of cleaning, why not become an expert in cleaning out garages? It's one of the most dreaded chores of all for homeowners. Offer to haul their trash and discarded items to the dump for an extra fee, or sell them yourself on Craigslist or at flea market.

PRESSURE WASHER: Many home owners dread the idea of pressure washing their house, walk or deck. Advertise your services, particularly at the places that rent the pressure washing machines. Rent a machine and power wash houses, decks, driveways etc.

CAR DETAILER: If you can wash, vacuum, wax and make old cars look new again, you can detail cars —

average price for car is $35 to $200 depending on how much work you are asked to do on it. A wash, vacuum and window/tire cleaning runs about $50 in small to mid-sized cities, and up to $100 or $150 in larger cities and for larger, luxury cars.

GUTTER CLEANER: Nothing lets home owners know they need their gutters cleaned like a good rain. Walk around after a hard rain and look for clogged gutters, then offer your services. With all the new devices used to clean gutters from the ground you won't even have to get on a ladder most of the time.

LEAF RAKER: Lots of retirees and people with disabilities and just plain busy people don't like raking their yards in the fall. Buy used leaf blowers and rakes for under $20 at thrift stores and hand out flyers, or post them in areas that get a lot of foot traffic. Talk to local hardware store managers. Many times their customers will ask them for a referral. Have a business card, or several cards you can leave at the store to hand out. Dog walker: Do you like animals? Consider becoming a dog walker. Take dogs to the local dog park, if your city has one, and make sure the dog gets its exercise — $15 to $35 an hour.

FINGERNAIL ARTIST: Fingernail artists generally work out of a salon, and like hair stylists they usually need a license to operate. Fortunately the training is usually less than a year and you can attend school while homeless.

DELIVERY PERSON: If you have a car advertise your services as a delivery person. You can charge people to pick up dry cleaning, packages, papers, equipment, etc. Make sure your insurance covers you and whatever you're delivering. In areas without fast food delivery you can charge $5-to-$10 plus tips to pickup and deliver food to businesses during lunch hour. The more meals you pick up and deliver to one place, the more you make.

HOUSE SITTER: (Sign up with www.housesittersamerica.com for $30 a year or www.mindmyhouse.com for $20 a year. Those are membership sites, not "find me a job" sites. For a list of most housesitting websites, go to http:// ultimatehousesittingguide.com/the-housesitting-directory-an-overview-of-all-major-housesitting-websites/)

WORK KAMPER: You can also find a place to stay free, along with paid work, at many campgrounds around the USA as a work camper. Some positions provide a free trailer for you to live in; others simply provide a campsite and hookups. Start with http://www.work-for-

rvers-and-campers.com/job-listings-for-RVers.html.
Here's an example of a work camping (sometimes
spelled "workamping") job listing:

Compensation: FHU and Salary (FHU means "Full
    Hook Ups" — water, sewer, electric)
Details:
Position Description: This is a year round position for
    a single or a couple. The successful applicant(s)
    will live on site and work full time. The camp
    ranger will be responsible for all aspects of camp
    maintenance, construction of new projects; cutting
    and splitting firewood; supervision of several
    seasonal employees; and will be responsible for
    responding to frequent after-hours repair / service
    calls during our busy summer season. For that
    reason, the camp ranger is required to remain on
    premises and be available for after-hours calls a
    minimum of 5 days per work week during the
    summer and 3 days per week during the winter
    months. The camp ranger will often deal directly
    with the public and must be courteous and
    professional in dealing with guests.
Compensation / Benefits:
- The Camp Ranger may provide his/her own RV or
    camping trailer up to 32' in length, OR the camp
    will provide very basic single occupancy living
    quarters.

*- Water / Electric / Sewer / Garbage / Phone / Internet
will be provided by the camp in addition to hourly
wages.*

*- Paid Time Off will be accrued at the rate of 8 hours
per 175 hours worked.*

*- Camp matches 100% of employee pre-tax
contributions to Simple IRA Plan retirement
account up to 3% of salary. (Employees are
automatically 100% vested)*

*- After 1 year of service, the camp ranger will become
eligible for profit sharing bonuses.*

*- Hourly wage (in additional to the above benefits) to
start at $12.00 per hour. (For additional details
visit our website.)*

Some work camping positions are part-time, 10-20 hours a week. Some require different duties, such as being an office manager, or grounds keeper only. These can be very good jobs, in the outdoors, casual dress and a great way to meet people. Find work at private and state campgrounds.

CONSTRUCTION CLEANUP: Go to job sites and clear out the trash, and do whatever the foreman needs to have done, not as an employee, but as a contractor. Recycle (for money) what can be recycled and sell scraps of whatever you haul away.

CLEANING OFFICE BUILDINGS: Smaller office buildings are often looking for good cleaners, small crews and consistent service. Having a night job (when most office cleaning is done) allows you to sleep days, especially good if you have a car to sleep in.

CLEANING HOUSES AND YARDS: While it's often easier to actually get a housecleaning job with a cleaning service, create your own business and specialize in cleaning yards. Many yards are in violation of county codes because of all the junk and trash in them, and you can get a list of those addresses from the county. Knock on a few doors or make a call and offer your services. Every city has its hoarders too. If you have the patience and stomach for cleaning, there is always a demand for cleaning. There are biohazard certifications for cleaning crime scenes and hoarder's houses. Make sure you have your shots up to date.

ORGANIZER: Professional organizers are in high demand. And while there are a lot of women in the field, why not be a male organizer specializing in helping men (or their wives) organize garages, attics, sheds and storage units? It's a job often given to husbands who don't want to do it, but women might love having a male organizer who can move big boxes and equipment.

LOADING OR UNLOADING COMMERCIAL TRUCKS: (Called a "lumper") Lumpers make between $60 and $500 for loading and unloading tractor-trailer trucks. In cities and larger areas lumpers are unionized, but in smaller towns and locations anyone who wants to be a lumper just has to talk to the dock foreman or the trucker.

MOVING HELP: You can load and unload for commercial truckers, or better yet, make up some business cards and leave them with the managers of self-storage facilities and places who rent U-Haul trucks. Many Do-It-Yourself movers welcome being able to hire someone to do the heavy lifting of boxes and furniture, and will pay well for it. Charge by the job, not the hour, to ensure that if you work hard and get the job done faster you make more money and that if you're slow; the customer doesn't feel taken advantage of. You don't need to have a vehicle. Do-It-Yourself types rent a U-Haul or have their own truck. You just need to get there. Many people will pick you up if help is hard to find.

TEACH SOMETHING: People make a business out of teaching others the things they know well, like bartending, or painting, or cooking a particular kind of ethnic food. Make a flyer and business cards and hand them out. Better yet, go to Michaels or other craft supply stores and sign up to teach a class there. If you know how to change the oil in a car, offer a basic car maintenance class for women on how to change the oil in their cars, or check their vehicle fluids. Do you know how to whittle? What can you do easily that other people might like to learn?

BAKE SOMETHING: There are churches and public kitchens that will rent you kitchen time to bake if you don't have your own kitchen. If you do have kitchen access, but not to a commercial kitchen, you can still legally sell your baked and canned goods at farmer's markets. Check the laws in your state about what you can /can't legally sell regarding food, but "Cottage Industry Laws" allow you sell most goods at farmer's markets without a certified or inspected kitchen. That doesn't mean you aren't liable if someone gets sick from your food, it just means the state and authorities won't shut you down for selling your homemade bread or muffins.

SELL SOMETHING: Go to the farmer's markets and see what is selling. Around the holiday time, things like Christmas items go fast. What can you make that no one else is making, or what can you make better?

I believe that anyone with the drive and ability to buy and read this book can do any of the jobs I've listed here. So, if you're reading this and thinking, "I can't do that. I'm not smart enough to do that," I'm telling you that you are smart enough and capable enough to start, run and succeed at your own business. Approximately 15 percent of the homeless that the vast majority of society sees are the addicts, the mentally ill, felons, pedophiles and alcoholics. Those are probably not the people reading this book.

The people reading this book are the 85 percent of people who are homeless because they lost their job, either through layoffs, firing or downsizing. They are used to working, are good workers and are looking for, but not finding, jobs where they are.

Readers reading this book may be on fixed incomes, not homeless, but close enough to see it becoming a reality if they don't make more money. So this is as much a guide to making short-term money fast as it is establishing an ongoing business. You can do many of these things as a business, or as a short-term money maker. It's up to you. Your success depends on you, and how smartly you apply what you learn here and how willing you are to persist.

No, it won't be easy. But it's no harder for you than it is for anyone else. Yes, you have the challenge of caring for yourself while homeless on top of other challenges, but you have the advantage of not having the overhead of other people too. It's a tradeoff, but one you can handle. Once you start making money and saving your money, you can afford a car or van to work out of, and then later a small storage unit, office or apartment.

Millions of immigrants come to America from around the world every year. They don't speak the language, or know the culture, or have a penny to their name, yet thousands of them start and run successful businesses, even becoming millionaires with a few years time. In fact,

Forbes Magazine says more than 10 percent of immigrants become billionaires in America. Immigrants are also four times more likely to become a millionaire than most Americans. Why?

ONE: They are savers, saving 15 to 20 percent of their income versus the 5 percent most Americans save.

TWO: They are risk averse. Rather than invest in stocks and ventures that promise 10 percent they invest wisely, settling for 2 to 5 percent return on their money.

THREE: They keep their expenses low. They don't go out and rent showy businesses, buy new cars or get sucked in by the trappings of wealth. They spend only what they have to spend to keep their business operating. Rather than rent an office and a house, they live together and work from the same space when possible. This means if you can work out of a car, or a Starbucks or your public library while you are getting started, then do it. If you don't absolutely need something, don't buy it.

FOUR: They are not materialistic. They don't need or believe in buying, owning and using every new gadget or device made. They ignore the temptation to buy name brand items, televisions, expensive apartments or cars.

Five: They reinvest their profits back into their business. If you decide to start out selling ice-cold bottle water and can only afford to buy a case at a time, you sell that case and take the $50 in profits you make and buy more water. You spend your profits on growing your business.

Starting a business is a lot like losing weight. The formula is simple: consume fewer calories than you burn and you'll lose weight. That part is simple. Doing it is hard. Starting a business is simple too — create a product or service people need and provide (see) it to them at a price that covers your direct and indirect costs and nets you a profit.

The next chapter goes into more detail about how to price your product or service, how to determine if your business idea is practical or how to determine how much money you can make by altering a few prices or numbers. As strange as it seems, bumping up the selling price of your items by 5 to 25 cents can often double your profits. "Break even" is the exercise you must do to determine your potential profits before you start your business. It will save you time, money and headaches to "crunch the numbers" on paper or in a spreadsheet before you start manufacturing or selling your services.

MARKETING: Marketing is the thing or things you do to promote your business and to sell your products or services. Marketing can include market research and advertising. It can be elaborate and expensive, or free and practical, or anything in between. "Market research" is a ten-dollar word for "what do real people think about your product or service?" Market research is as simple as just asking people what they like, or don't like, and what they'd like to see more of. If you don't have a market that wants your product or service pivot, and find something they do want.

If you don't have a storefront or fixed location where you're selling, it's very helpful to have business cards, postcards, flyers, posters or brochures to let people know what you can do for them. You also want to let people know how much you charge, as well as where they can find or contact you. Marketing is also part of your indirect costs and part of the cost of doing business. You can rely on word-of-mouth referrals for some businesses, but anything you can do to let people know about your business will help drive customers to you.

Advertising, public relations, drawing media attention and use of social media are all part of "marketing."

MEDIA ATTENTION AND PUBLIC RELATIONS

Media attention, or getting your story and the story about your new business in the newspaper, or on television or radio, can be a great sales boost. Getting media attention (television or newspaper or even blog coverage of your business) is part of marketing yourself.) t also raises awareness of your business. But that awareness boost only lasts a few days or weeks. Most media outlets will not keep telling readers about you once they have covered your story once. That's why they sell you ads.

To get that coveted media attention regularly; you have to have a great story, and a new story each time. One story may be about your starting your business. Another might be about the fact you were so successful you donated 100 turkeys to a local food bank a year after you got off the street.

Think about it. Who do you know who tells a good story? What's good about it? Chances are it's interesting, funny, different and told well.

What separates your business from other new businesses is your story and how you tell it. Your story is what makes you different from a business that just wants to attract customers. You can have a good story, but not tell it well. It's both an art and science to tell the kind of story that gets media attention.

In general, the media will want to know why your story is worth reporting on, or "covering." They may not be interested in your window washing business, but they may be interested in why you dress up in costumes that reflect the holidays to wash windows. That's different. They may be interested in hearing how you were homeless until you started your business, and now your business is doing so well you're in a new home.

The media usually aren't as interested in the business, as they are in the person running the business. Do you have an unusual story? Background? Former life as a millionaire who gave it all up to craft camping stoves out of soda cans? What is it that makes you and your company or business not only interesting but also different and better than your competitors? Did you have cancer and start your business to raise money for your treatment or the treatment of others? What is it you do that other people would find inspiring, funny, educational or different? That's the story the media will most likely want to hear you tell.

You get media attention in one of several ways:

A newspaper, radio or television journalist discovers you, either through using your service or hearing about you from someone else. They reach out to you and ask to do a story.

You tell the local media about your business with a press release. A press release is a one-page notice that tells the editor why your story would interest their readers. You don't tell them how awesome you are, or that they should do a story on you. You tell them something their readers would benefit from. Let's go back to the pooper scooping business, for instance. Your press release would have a catchy title that makes the reader want to read the press release. For example: "Top Three Things Pet Owners Hate Most about Their Pets." That will get their attention! Then you start the press release with what those things are, and you list "scooping up waste" as the top thing pet owners hate to do. They also hate to clean up hairballs and vomit. You offer several tips (research this on the Internet) about how to clean up pet messes and remove stains.

Remember, this is short, one-page story, about 300 words max. Then you put your company name and phone number on the release so the reporter can contact you if they're interested in running a story about you. Because you have just given them tips about something you do —

clean up pet messes — they consider you an expert and are more likely to contact you for more information. You'll need to have your name, email and phone number on the top of the press release. And, end it with, "If you'd like to know more about how pet owners can keep their yards clean and their pets healthy, call me."

Sometimes you need access to more reporters. So, go to www.helpareporter.com and sign up (free). This site, referred to as HARO (for Help A Reporter Out) sends out emails to business owners, public relations firms and individuals every day. They're looking for people to interview for stories. Each "pitch," as it's called, details what the reporter is looking for, who is a good candidate for the story and what you need to do to contact the writer.

The pitches have a time frame, usually of a day or several days before expiring. You need to act quickly to send them an email with the information they are asking for from readers. You may or may not be selected to be interviewed, but many people end up on national television after responding and being selected. You won't get paid to be interviewed and if you even ask about getting paid, you'll be dropped from consideration. What you will get is exposure for your business. So it's a good thing, something most companies pay thousands of dollars a month to get — media coverage.

You call or make an appointment to see the editor or a reporter and you pitch your story to them in person. This isn't a great way to go about it unless your business is unique and amazing. Journalists and editors are busy people and much prefer to read an email with your press release or "pitch" to them. If they decide not to run a story most will ignore you and not respond, but some will send you an email and say, "no thank you."

If you get rejected don't lash out, get angry, yell at them or be rude. Thank them politely and then wait for 30 days and try again with a different pitch about something else you do. I've had people with a decent story, but who contacted us (the newspaper) after we just ran a story like theirs.

We know our readers don't want to read another story about that topic so soon, so we declined their pitch. When they respond with cursing, threats and rudeness, they not only don't get their story, they are put on an unofficial "Never contact this jerk" list. You must be polite, pleasant and professional. There are a lot of reasons story ideas are rejected and the editor/reporter will rarely share that reason unless asked.

You can politely ask, but unless it was because they just ran a similar kind of story, the response you will most likely get will be, "It doesn't fit our editorial needs right now." That's an honest reply so accept it and try again in a month. Don't explode or yell at the editor or reporter. Be nice. Try again. You don't want to be shuffled to the "crazy, rude, demanding person" file. You'll never get any media coverage that way.

ADVERTISING: Once you have your business you'll need to advertise it. Advertising is the process of making or producing information (flyers, cards, ads etc.) that tell people what you're selling or offering. It's how you get the attention of potential customers and people who want and need your service or product.

If you need to create an ad, go to www.Canva.com. Canva is a free, online program that leads you through the process of designing your flyers and brochures and ads. You don't have to be a tech nerd to use it either. You can print off the file at your local library or through a friend's printer, or download the file and take it to a print shop where you can print off copies for about 8 to 15 cents per page, or more for color prints. You don't need thousands of copies. Print off 5 or 10 and place them in areas where you're most likely to get business. If you have a "pooper scooping" business, for instance, put a flyer at the entrances to parks and dog parks or trails — anywhere people who walk their dogs are most likely to see it. Hang one in a local pet store, or some place people buy pet supplies.

While everyone who wants to sell you ads will tell you that advertising is the best way to get new customers, the best way is word-of-mouth referrals from satisfied customers. When a customer uses your business or service and is pleased and happy with your work, they're more likely to tell a friend and refer other people to you. These are the referrals most likely to buy. Someone they trust who has vouched for you has referred them.

It's harder and more expensive to recruit new customers than it is to keep your existing customer base happy. So focus on your loyal customers and welcome new ones. Work the hardest to ensure your old customers keep coming back. How? For instance, let's say you clean gutters. Offer your existing customer half off for every new customer they refer to you that hires you. If you get two new customers who pay you full price, it's worth it to do one job (your existing customer) for free. Not only will your current customer feel good about a free gutter cleaning, but he'll also brag to his friends, and they'll want to do the same thing. It's like having a sales force working for you. Sit down and decide what your ROI (Return on Investment) is to make sure what you are offering isn't costing you more than what you're making.

These ideas are just the tip of the iceberg. Look around you. What do people need? What would make their lives easier? It may take you a while to figure it out, but you can do it. Millions have and you can too.

CHAPTER FIVE
The Business of Business

"Lack of money is no obstacle. Lack of an idea is an obstacle." ~ Anonymous

This chapter is about the basic information and tools it takes to start a business. For years I thought starting a business was a big deal, a scary thing that took brains, lots of money and a knack for numbers. Then someone pointed out to me that kids start businesses all the time — lemonade stands, mowing yards, raking leaves and even taking candy to school to resell at a markup to their friends.

If a 10-year-old can do it, so can you. As your business grows along the way you'll learn more about the complexities of things like tax structures, business structures, branding and marketing. To get started, however, all you need is an idea, and a basic plan — which I cover in this chapter. You'll need to understand what a "break-even" sheet is and how to determine if your idea will bring you a profit. It's not rocket science, and you can do it even if you don't have a college degree, or didn't finish high school. The five steps to business success aren't about being a business whiz. They're just common sense.

FIVE STEPS TO BUSINESS SUCCESS

REASEARCH: Thoroughly evaluating the market for your product is what will make you or break you. You have to know what people want and how to give it to them. You have to know what your competition is doing and how you can do it better. You have to understand your business.

PRIORITIZATION: Once you have the big vision about your idea and your business you'll start seeing smaller paths, other things that could add to or detract from your success. Friends and family will have their own ideas about how you should run your business, what you offer and how you should structure things. Listen to what they have to say, then ignore them and focus on what you want. There's nothing wrong with carefully considering other people's advice, but at the end of the day you are the one who will suffer the consequences of your decisions. If you were going to fail wouldn't you rather fail based on your own ideas rather than someone else's plans for your business? You have to focus and decide what you're doing — or not doing — with your idea. Tom was approached by several businesses that asked him if he would be willing to paint the inside of their stores, do carpentry work or janitorial cleaning. But Tom knew he wanted to be a window washing business, not a painting business, and he said, "No thanks." He knew to focus on his vision, not other's visions for him.

COMMUNICATING THE VISION: Tom knew clearly communicating the vision he wanted his business to achieve was critical. As long as Tom was the only employee, this wasn't a problem. As he hired employees it would become important to ensure everyone was working towards his original vision, that of being the best window washing business in the state. If his employees saw their jobs as just a means to a paycheck, or started trying to move in a direction not consistent with the company's vision, the business wouldn't work. Tom wanted customers to understand that he was first and foremost a window washer. Over time he would learn about all kinds of windows, and become something of a window expert too, but his focus was on window washing.

GREAT EMPLOYEES: No company succeeds without great employees. Finding, attracting and retaining a talented, committed and diverse workforce is what will keep your business growing. Tom learned to look for people with a work ethic and a personal pride in taking responsibility that matched his own. He could teach people how to wash windows. He couldn't teach people how to care about their jobs or own their mistakes. He took his time to find, recruit and pay the best people the best wages and his customers loved it.

DELIVER: The single most critical factor to business success is to figure out exactly what it is your customers want, and then deliver it better than they (or you) thought possible — and to keep doing that every day with every customer. Tom learned to spend a few minutes talking with each store owner to learn more about what was important to them, and how he could better serve them. Over time it would be those conversations with store owners that would help him develop an online scheduling system that allowed owners to schedule cleanings without having to talk to Tom directly.

Let's look at some simple examples:

A daughter of a friend of mine loved to sew. Her father saw how many of her friends were asking her to sew them fleece pajama bottoms, which was a popular item for teens in that rural area to wear to school. She hadn't been charging anyone to make the pajamas if they bought the materials. He saw a business opportunity for her, so he sat down with her and they figured out what it cost her to make a pair of pajama bottoms in terms of materials and time. He gave her a $50 loan to buy supplies, and then she started taking official orders. Ultimately it cost her $8 to make a pair of pants (labor and materials), so she sold them for $15 each.

Later she sewed other items like purses and bags. She did this throughout high school and used the profits to fund her college education. She learned how to start and run a business in the process. Her father was a businessman himself, so she had the advantage of his coaching and teaching. But you can learn what she learned. There are thousands of books and millions of pages on the Internet that will walk you through the process of starting your own business, no matter what that business is.

Starting a business is only as hard as you make it. If you over-think it, as I did when I started, you're going to struggle with it and be intimidated by it. If you see it for what it is — providing goods or services to others for a price — then it's not so scary.

There are 10 basic steps to starting a business. Don't let the list scare you. It's really not that complex. As a homeless person you'll have the same essential resources as most people, but you won't have the comfort, convenience or storage options a house or apartment offers. You may not have an income or money, but other than that, you do have what you need. It will be a little bit more challenging to start a business, but you can handle those challenges.

Thousands of immigrants come to America every year. Most have less than $10 in their pockets and don't speak English, yet they manage to start businesses and do very well for themselves. If you're one of those immigrants you can do this. That's the beauty of business. Anyone can do it.

Starting a business does involve some planning, financial decision making and jumping through some legal hoops The following 10 steps can help you plan, prepare and manage your business. The rest of the chapters in this book can make these steps easier to understand.

STEP ONE: Write a business plan. Don't worry; it's not as hard as it sounds. A business plan can be simple or complex. Let's do simple. A business plan is just a roadmap. It tells you where you want to go, and how you're going to get there, successfully. You will need to know:

- What your business is all about.
- What your company or business name is.
- What your product or service is.
- What it will cost you to produce your product or service (your break-even costs)
- Where you plan to get the money to start your venture.

Let's take an imaginary homeless man and call him Tom. Tom became homeless after losing his job, then his savings, then his apartment. He doesn't have a lot of job skills, but he wants to start a business. He had no idea what he could sell, but one day while sitting at the downtown mall he noticed a merchant washing the windows of his business.

"I could do that," he thought. So he decided to start a business washing windows. He knew that before he invested time and money into his idea, he first needed to create a business plan for himself. The business plan would tell him if the business was worth starting. He went to the library and used the library computer to Google, "How to clean commercial windows."

He wanted to learn what his new business idea was all about. He found hundreds of videos, like: https://www.youtube.com/watch?v=NSLu2uPxN84, and https://www.youtube.com/watch?v=FGKdmKX1z64. He noticed these videos explained some of the tips for washing windows correctly. He learned about different tools and how to use them, what products worked, and how to correctly wet and clean a window. He watched as many videos as he could, and decided window washing was something he could do. He decided to call his new business, "Tom's Window Washing." His service would be washing windows. He did some research and decided he could buy the basic tools he needed — a squeegee, sponge and rags, bucket and soap — for about $25. Once he got paid for a few jobs and made a profit he would invest that profit into better tools. Better tools would allow him to wash windows faster, which would allow him to wash more windows and make more money.

Tom had no idea how much he should charge for his services, so he got back online and Goggled, "How much should I pay for window washing?" He found a number of websites, including http://www.angieslist.com/articles/how-much-does-window-cleaning-cost.htm, which gave him various prices for professional window washing. along with several formulas for factoring how to give an estimate. He learned most cleaners charged by the pane, or square foot. Prices ranged from $2 to $7 per window pane. After reading several websites about what to charge, Tom did a *break-even* exercise to find out how much he needed to make an hour to break-even and then to earn a profit.

What is "break-even?" Break-even is the amount of money you have to earn selling your product or service in order to pay for the costs you invested in your product or service. For instance, a case of 50 cigarette lighters costs $12.49. You also have to factor in your labor, or if you're paying someone else to sell them for you, their labor. How much do you want to make an hour? Let's assume you want to make $10 an hour labor. You estimate it will take you three hours to sell 50 lighters. You plan to sell them on the downtown mall near a tobacco store you know charges $2.50 each for a similar lighter.

Now you've invested $12.49 in the lighters and $30 in

labor. Now you have to sell $42.49 worth of lighters to "break-even," or cover your investment in the lighters and pay you wages for three hours of your time. You can sell those lighters for $1 each, making $50, gross income. Gross income is the sum of all your sales before you take out wages, taxes and the cost of doing your business. You may want to sell them for $2, for a gross income of $100. One hundred dollars sounds like a great return, but now you need to factor in your costs to determine what your net profit is. Net profit is what you make after you deduct your costs from your gross income.

What are your costs? There's the $12.49 you paid for the lighters. Then there's labor, $30 for three hours work. So, subtract $30, plus $12.49 from $100. That leaves you with $57.51 in net profit. Remember, that $30 is wages, so you still walk away at the end of the day with $30 in earned wages, and $57.51 in profit, or $87.51 for your three hours of work. If you sell all your lighters in the first hour, your labor costs would be $10, and your profit would be $77.51.

Maybe you don't want to spend three hours selling lighters, or you don't have that much time. What if you have a job where there are a lot of smokers? Maybe you can sell your lighters at work. When someone forgets their lighter, or asks if you have a light, you can say yes, and sell them a lighter. You can charge more because they won't have anywhere else to go to buy a lighter while they're working.

Maybe you want to sell several items like lighters at a time. What if you set up a table at a tailgating party and sell lighters, cups, napkins, charcoal and lighter fluid? What is your break-even cost and potential profit then?

See how business gets more challenging? You've got to know exactly what your break-even cost is so you can effectively price your products in a way that you can make money. What if the tobacco store doesn't want competition and starts giving away lighters with every carton of cigarettes sold? If you are "priced out of the market" at that location, you may have to leave your spot and find somewhere else to sell your lighters where there is no competition. Or you'll need to find a way or a reason people will want to buy your lighters rather than your competitor's. Maybe you hire a pretty girl to sell your lighters, or you give away or sell a clip for the lighter that only costs you two cents to buy. You have to do something to make you stand out, something that makes you a more desirable merchant than your competition.

Tom had worked in an office and knew how to create spreadsheets. So he created a spreadsheet to help him figure out his break-even costs. If you don't know how to create a spreadsheet, go to our website and use the one we created. The website is: HomelessEntrepreneur.com:

Let's go back to Tom's business plan. Tom needed to know how much it was going to cost him to run his business. He needed to know his direct and indirect costs for starting and running his window washing business so he could determine if it was a good business idea.

After watching few videos about window washing to see what tools he would need, and then researching the cost of his tools and supplies, Tom learned his **direct costs** for each window washing job would be the cost of soap, water and rags, gas for his car and parking fees — about $8-$10 a day and his labor. The term "direct costs" refers to the materials, labor and expenses related to the production of a product or service. Tom also had *indirect costs* totaling about $100 a month. Those cost include business cards, advertising, and items related to keeping his business running whether he has a job lined up or not. He doesn't have an office, but he does work out of his car. So, he has car insurance, business insurance and the cost of cleaning his rags, buying soap and other items as he needs them.

Tom hadn't been paying his bills because he didn't have a job. But if he were to pay them, he'd need about $500 a month. That would cover his car insurance, gas and a gym membership so he could shower every day. He would take his food and campground fees, personal laundry costs etc. out of his personal profits.

Tom's indirect costs were the bills he had to pay every month to keep the virtual doors of his business open. Tom did two break-even sheets — one for his business and one for his personal cash flow situation. He learned he'd need to make a profit of at least $1,500 a month if he wanted to move into an apartment. He could keep living and working out of his van, which now cost him $500 a month. He wasn't sure he could make up that $1,000 difference he needed to get an apartment, so he decided to live in his van for at least another six months. He would save his money and then revisit his business plan and decide whether or not his business was successful enough for him to move into an apartment in six months, or sooner if business picked up.

Tom decided that he would need to clean at least 1,000 square feet of windows a month and charge at least $1 a square foot to break-even. His labor costs, or what he would pay himself, was $25 an hour (remember, he's paying taxes out of this wage too). He'd need to work 40 hours a month, or 10 hours a week to sustain his current living situation. He'd also need to work more hours promoting his business and selling his services, hours for which he wouldn't be paid directly.

This was what Tom called his "sweat equity." He learned his business idea was certainly viable. If he saved his money and worked enough hours he could easily be off of the streets and into an apartment in six months. The challenge would be to find enough businesses and homes willing to hire him. This awareness led to step two.

STEP TWO: Get business assistance and training. Getting assistance and training meant Tom needed to look around at the free training and resources, classes, counseling services and help available for him to make sure he was starting this business and running it effectively. There are organizations, nonprofits and online classes (many of which are free), which will help you prepare your business plan, get financing and find sources for making your product or services. They'll also help you learn how to market your business or service, create contracts and sell your product or service. This book is part of that training and assistance. Your local SCORE office (www.score.org) is another. Searching online for information on "How to start a business," and visiting the www.smba.org are other ways to find training and assistance for free, especially if you are in a rural area. You can also just ask a friend with a business for help.

Tom found his assistance online by watching YouTube videos about window cleaning, and by talking to a local SCORE volunteer. He took a few accounting classes to make sure he knew how to manage his business expenses, and to ensure he knew how to file taxes when the time came. He also learned about how to create a logo, a brand and how to market his services by watching videos and attending free SCORE classes and reading about business in books and online.

STEP THREE: Choose a business location. Where is your business audience? Who is most likely to want to buy your services or product? Tom lived in a rural area near a larger town with a downtown mall. Many of the stores in town had large plate glass windows that needed regular cleaning. Tom also found that a nearby retirement community could be a possible business opportunity because elderly residents simply could no longer get out to clean their own windows.

STEP FOUR: Finance your business. If you have a bigger business idea you're going to need more money. You can find government-backed loans, venture capital and research grants to help you get started, or you can borrow from friends and family, sell items you have in storage, cash in savings accounts or barter for what you need. Tom did some research and found he'd need less than $50 to finance his business, money he raised by finding items in dumpsters and selling them on Craigslist. It took him less than a day to raise the money he needed to buy his tools and the license fees he needed to get started.

STEP FIVE: Determine the legal structure of your business. Because Tom was both owner and employee, he opted to be a sole proprietor. When things got bigger and better he would become an LLC (cost = $100). For now he was content to be a sole proprietor.

You may want to explore other options to determine which form of ownership is best for you: sole proprietorship, partnership, Limited Liability Company (LLC), corporation, S corporation, nonprofit or cooperative.

SOLE PROPRIETORSHIPS: Sole Proprietorships are usually owned by a single person or a couple. You're personally liable for all business debts, can freely transfer all or part of the business, and, for taxes, you can report profit or loss as personal income.

LIMITE LIABILITY COMPANIES (LLCs): Limited Liability Companies (LLCs) are very popular too. You have limited legal liability like a full corporation; however, for taxes they're more like Sole Proprietorships or Partnerships.

GENERAL PARTNERSHIPS: If you're doing business with a partner or group, general partnerships let you share profit, loss and managerial duties among the business partners. This means each partner is personally liable for any debt entirely. Members file an informational tax return and income/loss is filed personally. ("Joint Ventures" are short-term partnerships.)

There are "C corporations" and other designations for larger companies. There are thousands of websites that debate the pros and cons for every kind of business structure, but almost all agree that for a small business just starting out, a sole proprietorship is the way to go.

STEP SIX: Register your business name with the state government. This cost varies from $10 and up depending on what state, city and county you're in. You'll need an address to do this, so before you file those papers, rent a post office box, or ask a family member or friend if you can use their address as your residence.

STEP SEVEN: Get a Tax Identification Number. You can use your Social Security Number (SSN), but since you'll be using it to purchase supplies, etc. it's best to have a Tax ID to protect your SSN. Tax ID numbers are free, even though there are dozens of websites happy to charge you $100 and up to do what you can do for yourself. To get your FREE Tax ID number find out what kind of number you need, and then fill out the forms through the IRS website: https://www.irs.gov/Businesses/Small-Businesses-&-Self-Employed/Apply-for-an-Employer-Identification-Number-%28EIN%29-Online

It's a simple process, but you must complete it in one sitting — usually about 15 minutes. If you land on a website that wants to charge you for an Employer Identification Number (EIN) which is your tax number, you're on the wrong site. EIN numbers are free.

STEP EIGHT: Register for state and local taxes. Yes, you have to pay taxes. You can probably get by with not doing this for a few weeks while you decide if you really want to go into business for yourself. but any income over $600 must be reported to the IRS. If your income for the year falls below $9,750 and you're under 65 years old, or below

$11,200 if you're over 65 years old, you still need to file a tax return, but chances are you won't be paying income tax.

Register with your state to obtain a tax identification number, workers' compensation, unemployment and disability insurance.

STEP NINE: Get your business license and permits. Tom learned that he needed to have a cleaning business license called a "Service Contractor's License."

Before he could get licensed, he had to be "bonded," which meant applying for a license bond.

Step 1. File a "Doing Business As" or business license application with your local municipal government and open a business bank account. Some banks require you to be an LLC to open a business account, others don't.

Step 2. Check the Small Business Administration's Licenses and Permits page to see if you are required to have a cleaning license to work in your area.

Step 3. File necessary applications to become a licensed cleaning business.

Step 4. Contact insurance companies about a License Bond and a Surety Bond.

There are two kinds of cleaning bonds that a building / janitorial services or window washing company might need to have:

License and Permit Bond. You'll only need these bonds if your municipal government licenses you. Local governments can be sued if they license a contractor or cleaning professional who does poor work. These bonds protect the municipal government from the cost of a lawsuit.

Janitorial Bond / Housekeeper Surety Bond. Often referred to as a surety bond or contract bond, these bonds reimburse clients who pay for a service they never receive. If a cleaning business fails to deliver the work it promised, the Contract Bond reimburses the client for the fees they spent. In essence, these bonds help secure and enforce contracts. These are pretty affordable bonds — usually about $100 a year.

License bonds and cleaning services bonds offer more than just financial coverage. They are a way for you to reassure clients that you are a professional and that you can reimburse them for problems with your work.

Most clients want this assurance that you're bonded and licensed before they will hire you. Tom was fortunate because in telling people he knew about his new business, several small businesses agreed to hire him without a bond. Tom went back and factored the cost of the bond and fees into his break-even sheet.

STEP TEN: Know your Employer Responsibilities. Tom was both sole employee and company owner, so he didn't worry about what he needed to know to hire employees. That would come in a few months when he found demand for his services increasing to the point he needed to hire employees to keep up with the demand. In the meantime, he could push that concern aside. You may or may not ever hire employees. You may want to start a business with a spouse or partner. But you should know that as you grow, and if you are to grow, at some point you'll need to hire employees. So start thinking about that and reading about how to find good employees before you need them.

STARTING YOUR BUSINESS: The process of starting a business *begins* with coming up the idea for what product or service you want to sell. Tom found his ideal business, and you will find yours. I used to think business owners had a hobby or passion and they started there, turning their passion into a business. But then I learned that a majority of people simply enjoy the business of business and don't really care what they sell as long as it's making them money. I love writing so I turned my passion for writing into a business writing books for people.

Hope Lawrence, co-owner and founder of Henry Hudson Baking Company, for instance, didn't have any particular passion. She just wanted a business that would allow her to stay home with her two sons and her husband. She started thinking about what kind of business she could start in order to do that. She thought about what she liked, and what would be viable for her situation. She decided that since she liked to bake, baking something would be a good business. Eventually she settled on baking granola because it was easy to make, people liked it, it had a long shelf life and it wasn't as much work as muffins, cakes and bread. Hope started selling her granola at a local farmer's market. It was great granola and word spread fast about her product. It's a premium priced granola, selling for $2-$3 more than store brands, yet it sold well, and soon she found herself going from a one-woman operation to an eight-person operation that she runs with her husband.

According to *Success Magazine,* in 1994, at age 30, Jeff Bezos — then the youngest senior vice president of D.E. Shaw, a Wall Street hedge-fund firm — read a report projecting annual Internet growth at 2,300 percent. To a Princeton graduate in electrical engineering and computer science, "that was a huge wake-up call about the potential of the Web," Bezos said in the article. Three months later he walked away from his job and set out west in an aging Chevy Blazer with his wife, MacKenzie, driving and their golden Labrador in the back.

As the myth goes, by the time the trio reached Seattle, Bezos had written the initial draft of a business plan on his laptop, retained a lawyer by cell phone and started the search for a vice president of development. Five days later they moved into a rented house in the suburb of Bellevue, set up shop in the garage and voila! Amazon.com, the online retailer that now bills itself as Earth's Biggest Bookstore, was born.

Prior to his epic cross-country road trip, however, Bezos had done three months of research, drawing up a list of 20 items he could potentially sell. He had no particular interest in books. He just knew the Internet was going to be a great way to sell lots of items and he wanted to get as many SKU (unit numbers) numbers online as he could. There were thousands of office supplies he could sell, and thousands of clothes too. But the thing that eventually convinced him to sell books was the fact that there were millions of books, and millions of SKU numbers. People who bought books from Amazon knew exactly what they were getting — a book is a book is a book. Whether you buy a copy of John Grisham's latest bestseller at Amazon or at your local bookstore, you know what you're getting. So Bezos' plan called for selling books. He has expanded his online bookstore to include millions of other items now, but he began with a simple business plan he wrote to sell books.

The whole point of this is that business is its own animal. You don't have to have a hobby or passion or some special skill set to start a business. You just have to want to make money selling a product or service to someone else. How well you end up doing that will determine your success, but the fact is, that is what business is all about.

The most important thing about starting a business is not the idea. Ideas are easy. Ideas are a dime a dozen. Millions of people have a great idea. The value comes in executing your idea. The hard part of starting a business is in making your idea work.

CHAPTER SIX

Finances — Making, Saving, Investing and Managing Your Money

"Money is only a tool. It will take you where you want to go, but it will not replace you as the driver." ~ Aynn Rand

You're homeless either by choice or because you have no money to pay for housing and the related bills to maintain an apartment or house. If you have money you can use it to solve your problems — simply rent an apartment, hotel or house. If you don't have money, well then, you don't have a whole lot of choices. Money can't buy happiness, but it can make shopping for it a lot easier. You know when you have an income you have choices. The bigger the income, the more choices you have. It's simple. And when you don't have money, and don't know when it's going to come in, there is no bigger stressor.

Once you start a business and start making a little bit of money, even if it's $20, $100 or $500, chances are you're going to feel pretty darn excited and tell yourself you "deserve" to treat yourself. Whether it's new shoes, a case of beer, a new coat, etc., you're probably going to spend it on something that makes you feel better. Heck, I did. The first $115 I made on a freelance job in 2008 I went out and bought $114 worth of groceries. Not smart food that would last, but steak and stuff I wanted. I blew it, and the next few paydays I had, on food. Then the rent and bills came due and I didn't have the money to pay them. I had eaten all my profits. I ended up moving out of my apartment and in with a friend before I got evicted. I lost my deposit. I felt like a failure. I hadn't saved a dime.

Later, when my laptop crashed I didn't have money for a new one. I was still spending all my checks as soon as I got them. I was living paycheck to paycheck. These were small checks — $40, $75 — and I didn't think they were large enough to save anything, even as little as $5.

I should have been squirreling at least 20 percent of them away, saving for the rainy day that was coming. But I didn't. No one ever taught me to do that. I ignored any common sense that tried to get my attention. And I paid dearly for it.

Once you start making money you don't have to save it all, but you do need to save some of it. Some has to go for taxes, some for additional business purchases and some for a rainy day fund — for when you need to buy more

154

supplies, or fix your car, or take advantage of a great buy on something you really need, like a van, or a cheap apartment, or a down payment on something that will help you expand your business. Maybe you've been selling ice water out of a crappy $2.50 Styrofoam cooler. Take $2 or $10 from your profits and put it towards a sturdy, heavy duty cooler you can roll around instead of one that falls apart when loaded with ice and water. Invest in yourself and your business.

To manage your money you've got to have a plan. You can try to operate without a plan, but that's not the best way to run a business that will make you the money you want. You have to know where your money is coming from and where it's going. Your money also needs a job. Yes. A job. Part of its job is to be savings. Part is to pay you. Part of its job is to buy supplies for the business. You have to allocate money where it will be your friend. I tithe 10 percent, save 20 percent and set aside 25 cents on each dollar for taxes. I also pay myself a salary after that. There's not a lot of money let over after I do that, but what there is goes into my business account where it's used to buy the things I know I'll need — like office supplies, software and things I have to have to run my business. I long for the day when I have enough money for a new computer or camera, but because I'm saving, I know those days are coming. I have a plan for my money. I know where I want it to live and I make my money sure it finds its way to the right home before I blow it on stuff I want, but don't need.

My salary goes into the bank and is spent according to my spending plan (budget) on rent, phone, insurance, etc. I found out the hard way if you don't manage your money, it will manage you. Even if you're homeless, and especially if you're on a fixed income, it's important you know your personal break-even numbers. How much money do you have to make a month to pay your expenses? Maybe the only expenses you have are laundry, showers and food. You don't have rent. Maybe you do have rent, Internet, a car and insurance. How much do you have to make to pay all your indirect costs (bills that come due every month no matter what) each month?

How much rent do you pay? Internet? Phone? Car? Gas? Food? Until you know exactly where your money is going, you can't direct it to the best place it can be. You can't make your money work for you if you're sending it out the door to play the minute you get paid.

I was, and still am, terrible with money. If I have it, I tend to spend it. It takes a lot of discipline to save and to pay bills before doing anything else with it. But I'm working on it. The first step was coming up with a break-even for my personal finances. How much money did I need to make to pay my bills every month? That includes how much did I have to have for my rainy day fund (three to six months of living expenses in case I couldn't work for that long), my emergency fund (what if the computer breaks?) and my retirement? That included a tithe (10 percent) and my $5 fun money. (I always save $5 for a fun fund. Once it gets to a respectable level I use it to buy myself something I want, or to go do something I want to do.

That break-even ranges from $800 to $1,800. I never ever let my rent or utilities get behind. I have no desire to become homeless again, so I know that even if I don't pay another bill I will pay rent and utilities so I have a place to live. My car is paid for, and I can restrict my costs by not driving as much as I might want to. I also pay my Internet and phone bill. Those are how I make my living.

When I can, I pay my rent and utilities in advance, earning a credit each month and taking the strain off of monthly bills.

Everyone has their own methods. What matters is that however you manage your money, you manage your money. That means a savings account, or a prepaid credit or debit card where you can add money to your account. Figure out a way to divide your money into accounts. Many homeless people carry wads of cash on them. I don't advise this for obvious reasons. Open a savings account, or get a safe deposit box, or rent a storage unit and hide it in envelopes in your belongings ... whatever works, but save it, manage it and know where it's going. Money is a resource, a tool. Without it you can't run a business because you won't have the cash flow to buy the products or things you need. The number one reason small businesses fail is inadequate cash flow.

There are thousands of resources on the Internet for learning about money management, but they all boil down to three simple principles:

SAVE AS MUCH AS YOU CAN

Know exactly how much it costs you to live every month and where your money goes; and

Have a plan for every dime you make, either salary, taxes, business, expenses or rent, every dollar you make should have a designated place to go and it should go there no matter what.

Looking back at my times of homelessness I can see now that not managing my money, not saving, not putting something — even a dollar or two — away for a rainy day (because every day felt like a hurricane to me) was my biggest mistake.

I know it feels like someone will take it, or steal it, or it will disappear or be garnished or something if you open a bank account. So many people are after you for money because you owe so many for so much. It's just more secure to keep it in your pocket. However, there are ways to save, and to protect your money. Use debit cards, like the Wal-Mart card. Some cards, like GreenDot or NetSpend, let you set up a separate savings account on your card so you can save for something special without being able to access your savings from the card. You have to go online and transfer money out of that savings account into your debit account before you can spend it. It's not a failsafe process, but it can greatly cut down on impulse spending.

If you want to save, simply buy a card — again, I like Wal-Mart's card because of their low rate ($3), free direct deposit and no monthly fees. Load or add on money to the card as often as you like. You can spend it like a bank debit card when you need to, or withdraw money out of an ATM as needed. The goal is to save money and avoid garnishments.

Another good thing about prepaid cards is that you can hide them on your person easier than you can cash. I used to keep several $50 cards in my van for emergency gas purposes. If you bought this book for a homeless friend, I urge you to consider giving it to them with several gift cards for restaurants, fast food, gas stations (if they have a car) and even shower tokens from local truck stops, or a gift membership to Planet Fitness ($10 a month).

I am not a financial advisor, and I'm not giving financial advice. I'm saying that if you want to get your life under control, you need to get your money under control.

Put aside 10 percent of everything you make. If you make $5 helping someone load something into their car, put 50 cents in savings. I started doing something like this with loose change and another with coins I found on the street. I'm not rich. I'm a paycheck-to-paycheck person myself. So I started just emptying my pockets into a jar at the end of every day. I didn't even count it. I just dumped it in this jar.

When one client had to push payment back, and another cancelled their job, I literally got down to a $10 bill in my pocket. I dug into that jar and counted out all the change from two months of dumping coins into it. I had more than $50 — enough to get me through until my next payday. The jar with coins I find on the street, mostly dimes and pennies, has almost $4 in it. Not much, but we're talking money I find on the street — and I live in a very rural area!! These are my two simple "mad money" systems. I usually take the contents to the bank and put them in my savings account, but sometimes I just consider it part of my rainy day fund and use it for gas or groceries.

The point I'm trying to make is have some kind of system to save. It should, for all practical purposes, be a savings account, but if you don't trust banks, or want to avoid having your savings garnished, then by all means use a jar, a debit card, an envelope system or something that will allow you to save.

You can also pay bills in advance. If you have a prepaid cell phone, did you know you can save money by paying 3, 6 or 12 months in advance? When I pay a year's rent in advance I get a free month tacked on — 13 months for the price of 12. I save $60 a year paying my auto insurance for the year instead of incurring a $5 surcharge by paying it monthly. I recently made $40 by calling AAA, the auto insurance and roadside assistance company. I called with a question about my insurance and the operator told me I got a discount by having both AAA roadside assistance and

AAA auto insurance. I said, "I already have both. Do I still get my discount?" The answer was yes, so now I have a $40 refund coming my way. It will go into savings since I consider it "found money" and not income.

There are a lot of ways to save money, cut back on costs and use what you save to invest in a business. It all depends on how important having a business is to you. If it's important, you'll find a way. If it's not, you'll find an excuse.

HAVE A SPENDING PLAN. You need a spending plan, which is a budget essentially, but I hate the word budget. So come up with a plan. Have some idea of what money you have coming in every month, how much you are spending and what you're spending it on. Savings should be a big part of your plan. It may be hard to save now, but you'll be glad you did later down the road.

Give your money a "job." Make sure every dollar is accounted for. Put money into plain old envelopes labeled with what you plan to spend the money on. These envelopes may say "gas" or "insurance" or "new socks and shoes," but that's okay. Having to sort it out and see, touch and relate to what you're spending it on will help you learn how to manage it.

GIVE BACK. Yes. I know it's hard to give money to someone else when you're homeless too, but think of it like this — there is always someone worse off than you are. When you give or help others, the people above you on the food chain are moved to help you. It's not that they see what you're doing, but God, or the universe or whatever faith you have, moves to reward you. I like to call it God, but whatever works for you. It's just a law of the universe, like gravity. So give 10 percent of what you make, with gratitude and a generous heart, and it will come back to you somewhere along the way. I guarantee it.

That said ... Here's the thing. If you haven't discovered this hard fact already, let me share it with you. You are the only one who is going to pull yourself out of your current situation. Others may or may not help, and most won't. You are your best lifeline. How are you going to get yourself out of this? **Hint:** By earning money and saving as much money as it takes, and being as generous and giving as often as possible. It's true and you know it. Now it's up to you.

CHAPTER SEVEN

Boundaries — What They are, Why You Need Them

"The first thing you need to learn is that the person who is angry at you for setting boundaries is the one with the problem." ~ Drs. Cloud and Townsend, Boundaries

Chances are, if you're homeless you have poor, weak or inconsistent boundaries. I can't point to a study or any definitive proof that that is the case. It's anecdotal. I've just seen that quality — poor boundaries — in a lot of the homeless I've encountered, including myself. Poor boundaries can include boundaries that are too rigid or limits that are poorly communicated.

So what is a boundary and what does it have to do with business anyway? The purpose of having boundaries is to protect ourselves from others and how they treat us. Boundaries let people know how we expect do be treated. Boundaries aren't about manipulating others to get them to do things they don't want to do. They're about communicating what is okay, or not okay, in how we are treated. I don't like to work after 9 p.m., so I tell my clients my hours are between 8 a.m. and 8 p.m. They know that I don't work after that. They don't call me because they know I won't answer. That's a boundary around my time.

Clients know if they want me to work over the weekend they'll pay extra because my weekends are work-free too. Some clients push me to work anyway because they want things faster. Others offer more money for me to work outside my stated hours. If the money is important to me and I feel like working, I can choose to change my boundary, or not. Healthy boundaries are also flexible. We can keep some people out and let others in. Just as we have a door on our homes (a physical boundary), and can let friends in and keep out strangers, our emotional, mental, spiritual and social boundaries are the same way. We can decide where, when, why and how we'll change our boundaries according to how we feel and what we want.

Boundaries are the edges or limits of something. For instance, yards have fences. Countries have borders. Even in social settings, or public transportation or restrooms, there are common boundaries around where it's okay to sit or stand, or how closely you can crowd another person's personal space before they get angry. While being six inches away from someone's face might be okay on a New York Subway train packed with commuters, or in Saudi Arabia, or at an intimate dinner party, it's not okay in an office, on the streets or in other public settings. Human beings like their physical space and go to elaborate ends to communicate that — either by setting their luggage on the seat next to them in an airport, or on a bus, or by spreading out or withdrawing when seated in public, like on a park bench. Others communicate verbally, "Would you step back a foot or two? I need a little more space to feel comfortable."

The message is clear — keep away, leave me alone. Boundaries also tell people how we expect to be treated and what we'll do if we aren't treated as we've asked. That doesn't mean people have to treat us the way we want, but it does tell them what we want.

My friend Mary doesn't like for people to raise their voice when speaking to her. She's in a wheelchair. She had an automobile accident that left her a paraplegic. She laughs about how often people speak to those in wheelchairs as though they're deaf or brain damaged, and not paralyzed.

"I tell people, I'm a paraplegic. My legs don't work, but my ears do. I am not deaf or brain damaged," she says. However, if she doesn't speak up and let people know how she feels and wants to be treated, people tend to treat her as an invalid or worse. "I want them to see me as a person and respect me as a professional," she said. By communicating her boundaries — "Please speak to me in a normal voice, and either sit down or squat down to look me in the eyes," she says. "Having to bend my head back to look up at you is painful." She's polite but very specific. She has to be.

She is teaching people how to treat her. When people insist on treating her like a cripple, or with pity, she simply says, "I don't think you understand my condition. I can't walk, but I'm still a professional, and I expect to be treated like one." For those who can't do that, she doesn't engage with them. She respects herself too much to be treated with pity or disrespect. She doesn't try to get other people to change; she uses her boundaries to protect herself. When she needs help she asks for it. She has learned to be very specific about what she wants or doesn't want so she gets what she needs. Having good boundaries makes her life much easier.

John, a wheelchair-bound colleague of Mary's, is the exact opposite. John refuses to ask for help when he's in a store or to tell people around him what he needs. As a result, he tends to blow up and scream at people when his frustration is greater than he can bear. People don't know how to respond because his boundaries are inconsistent or non-existent.

Sometimes it's okay to push his wheelchair, sometimes it's not. He doesn't let people know when to push or not, so people tend not to push him when he'd like them to help. This frustrates him and makes him angry. People can't read his mind, and he's unable to verbally express his needs, so he tends to be unsatisfied with people.

When he does let people know what he needs or wants, he has let his frustration build until his requests come out as rude demands. He then gets even more angry and frustrated that he scares people away with his anger. John has never learned to set, express or enforce healthy boundaries. He believes he's not worthy of respect, and that's pretty much what he gets — no respect. He has taught people to treat him as a human bomb. Not having healthy boundaries makes our lives harder for us and for others who never know how to treat us. They don't know how to treat us because we don't really know how we want to be treated. To know what you want, and what you don't want, you need to take time to think about how you want to be treated, then you need to communicate that clearly and effectively.

One of my boundaries is that I expect people to be on time if they've asked me to meet them for lunch or business. When I schedule business meetings, I'm usually 5 to 10 minutes early. That gives me time to find parking and find the venue if it's new to me. I also have time to use the restroom, comb my hair, find a good seat or table and get comfortable before my client or appointment arrives. I understand that many people are consistently happy to breeze into an appointment 15 minutes late. However, they won't be late with me for no good reason more than a couple of times because I don't tolerate it.

I think being late to an appointment shows disrespect. When a person is late the first time I'll express concern, "I was getting worried. I thought you might have been in an accident. I would really appreciate it if you're going to be delayed next time if you'll call or text me." The second time they're late I'll say, "I'm sorry you're late. That's going to cut in on our time together because I have to leave in 30 minutes. Hey, is this something that happens a lot? Your being delayed? It's disappointing for me because I enjoy your company, but I really hate it when people consistently show up late. How can make sure that doesn't happen again? Maybe meeting on a different day or at a different time would be better?" I don't want to punish the person. I just want to ensure my time is respected and they are able to meet with me without hurting their day. Boundaries aren't meant to be punishment. They're meant to help you and the person you're expressing them to find a way to make things work for both of you. Sometimes that's not always a possibility. That means you can choose to adjust your boundaries, or walk away.

I bring up the boundary of time because it's a fairly common issue. I know that many people assume if they're 15-20 minutes late that you'll automatically accommodate them and extend your time with them to make up for the time they were late. This shows they don't value or respect your time, only theirs.

I recently agreed to meet with a potential client at 8 a.m. We were both going to be attending the same 9 o'clock lecture at a conference. So, we decided to get there early and talk before the workshop started. However, he didn't show up until halfway through the workshop. He waved at me, but made no attempt to text, or talk with me as we'd agreed to. I left 10 minutes before the lecture was over because I had another appointment. He later called to ask why I hadn't stayed after the talk to speak with him. This wasn't the first time he'd been late or a no-show. I told him I couldn't work with him and explained why. I need to have clients show up and keep commitments or my schedule is thrown off by my trying to accommodate them. Boundaries ensure you respect your own time as well. He wanted to work with me enough that he promised to change.

Knowing it's hard for anyone to change that quickly, I tied a cost into it. He would deposit a retainer fee with me and every time he stood me up or was late, it would cost him. After spending the entire $500 worth of "late fees" in a few months, he actually did improve and was never late again. He learned to adjust his behavior because he had an financial incentive to do so, at least with me. I got paid for my time and the hours I spent waiting on him to show up. So I was happy.

Back when I was a massage therapist for a few years I had a few clients consistently arrive 30 minutes late for a one-hour massage. They expected me to give them a full hour's work, even though they were late. They expected this because other massage therapists they'd had, who didn't have firm boundaries, let them do this. So they assumed all massage therapists were as flexible.

I charged them for the full hour, gave them the rest of their hour (which usually was 10-15 minutes after they got changed) and reminded them that it was their hour and how they chose to use it (sitting in traffic or chatting with someone at work when they should have been driving) was up to them. Their inability to schedule their day so they arrived on time was their responsibility, not mine. If they wanted to see me again, however, they had to pay me for the hour they booked whether they showed up or not. I explained I had clients coming in after them and that I respected their time too.

I made allowances for traffic accidents they'd been in or family emergencies, like a death or trip to the emergency room for their child, etc., but after paying for an hour they didn't get to use, most clients were never late again. My boundary was, I expect to be paid in full for time of mine someone books. I can't get that time back. It's gone. I value my time, so I set boundaries around it. I've missed appointments and have been billed for them, so I quickly learned how painful that can be.

Surprisingly enough, they didn't argue and agreed to my boundaries. They just needed to know how I expected to be treated, what my policies were and if I'd enforce them. Eventually I wrote down my policies (boundaries) and gave each new client a copy their first time. It practically eliminated any issues I had after I started doing that.

How are Boundaries Different from Manipulation?

Isn't that manipulating someone to tell them if they don't do something we'll punish them? Well, we're not punishing anyone. We're telling them how we'll respond when they treat us a certain way. It's still up to them to make their own choice. If I say, "If you keep yelling at me I'm going to end this conversation and leave." It's up to the person yelling at me to decide if they want to keep yelling or not. They now know that if they do keep yelling, I'll leave. They get to make the choice about whether they want me there more than they want to yell. They are in control of their behavior, and its consequence. I am in control of my behavior and its consequence. Maybe this person yelling at me is a customer and I'll lose a sale if I walk away. I have to choose whether not being yelled at is more important than potentially angering the customer. Personally? I choose my own comfort over that of a customer who is yelling at me.

Boundaries aren't manipulation because, when we set a boundary, we let go of controlling, or trying to control, the outcome. We don't fret and worry about whether the person will honor it or not. If they do, great. If they don't, well, that's when we implement consequences. If someone consistently shows up late to appointments with me, they must either pay me in advance or I stop working with them.

I have a good friend who smokes. I hate the smell of tobacco and tell people they can't smoke in my car (boundary). My friend complains that she can't smoke in my car, and I refuse to ride in her car because she smokes there. We now drive places separately. My boundary around people smoking in my car is intact. When we recently went on a long road trip she agree not to smoke in the car if we stopped every so often so she could get out of the car and smoke. Boundaries don't mean people have to do everything your way, they give you a point where you get what you need/want and also offer a point to negotiate around their needs as well.

For a year I had a client pay me for an hour of coaching every week. He'd schedule the time, then never show up because he had other things come up. He was a CEO of a large company and he understood that people's time is valuable. We talked about it and he said he was happy to pay for the hour, but that sometimes he wouldn't be able to be there. He agreed to call and let me know as soon as he as he knew he couldn't make it. That gave me the option of taking on another client at that time, in which case I didn't charge him for the time. It worked well for us both.

So boundaries are also about taking the responsibility to take care of ourselves. If you're a business owner you need time for yourself. If you say yes to everyone and everything, you'll soon burn out. Boundaries help you protect yourself, your energy and your time. You decide whether you will do or not do something, or if you will go along with someone else's demands. As a business owner, you may be asked to lie, cheat or steal. If you have healthy boundaries around ethics, your boundary would be, "I have a policy of obeying the law, no matter how lucrative breaking that law might be. If you insist on dealing illegally or cheating or lying about _____, then I can no longer do business with you." And then you walk away.

Learning to set boundaries is critical to communicating to others and ourselves that we have worth. If you don't feel like you have worth, it's going to be very hard to start and run a successful business. If you don't value yourself, others won't either.

There are basically three parts to a boundary. The first two parts have to do with actually setting the boundary. The third part is about what we will do to defend the limit we've set. Setting a boundary has to do with deciding what your boundary is. For instance, I have a boundary of never loaning anyone money. I may feel like giving someone the money they need, but I never loan it. Those few people I do loan it to are people close to me who have a relationship of some kind with me, and whom I'm invested in. So my boundary is, "I don't loan people money." So, one day a vendor I work with, but don't know very well, came to me and asked to borrow a large sum of money, the equivalent of his paycheck, for a week. He assured me that he'd pay me back on Friday when he got paid. I'm thinking if he pays me back this entire amount on Friday he won't have any money for the following week and will just borrow more money, and never get caught up. I see that he is in financial trouble, but his financial problems are not my responsibility. They're his. I have a boundary, and a policy of not loaning people money, so I tell him, "I see it's rough not having money when you need it, however, I have a policy of not loaning people money." He continued to insist, arguing that I had the money, and that I could spare it. He continued to badger me to loan him the money.

So I expressed my boundaries again:

When you continue to ask me to loan you money after I've said "No" I feel angry. (This is a description of the behavior I find unacceptable.)

I also feel annoyed that you're continuing to bug me about loaning you money after I've said 'No.". (This describes how I feel.)

If you continue to ask me for a loan, I'll have to stop using you as a vendor because this is an inappropriate request. It's up to you. This is the last time I'll say "No." Next time you ask I'll stop taking your calls or emails. (I describe what action I will take to protect and take care of myself if he continues to violates my boundary.)

If he still continues to beg for money or berate me for not loaning him the money, I don't get into an argument or beg him to stop. I do exactly what I told him I would do: I stop taking his calls and emails and I stop using him as a vendor. I'm not trying to manipulate him. This is not a power struggle. It's pure and simple boundaries. I let go of the outcome, let go of hoping he'll leave me alone and I let go of worrying that he won't like me if I say no. I know what my boundaries are, I communicate them clearly, I communicate the consequences and I enforce both as needed. That said, I am not successful every time. No one is. He can choose to stop asking to borrow money and get to keep his contract with me, or not. It's his choice. He now knows what the consequences of his actions will be, and he gets to choose which action to take. No manipulation there!

It sounds simple, but it's hard to implement. It's also necessary if you are to have a successful business. Clients and customers will try to manipulate you and badger you, vendors will treat you like a doormat, and you'll spend more time feeling frustrated and cheated than it's worth.

Boundaries can be a difficult concept to grasp, but they're critical if you want to succeed at business — or in life.

Example: Pretend you run a fast food franchise. You've hired a teenager who has been pretty responsible and a good worker. He's only been working for a week or so. One day you see him giving his friends free sodas. What do you do? You communicate your boundaries and your business policies about work.

"I noticed you giving away free sodas to your friends. Those sodas cost me money. I know you want to be liked and be cool, but do not give away any more sodas. I expect you to pay for the three sodas you just gave away. If I see you doing that again, I will fire you." Put this down in a short letter and have them sign it, indicating they understand the policies and the consequences if they violate them again.

Then the next time the employee gives away food or sodas, remind them of the consequences you expressed earlier, and fire them. By doing that, you're teaching your employees what kind of behavior you expect from them.

What if your business is selling hot dogs? One day you notice your hot dog bun vendor taking buns from the week-old pile in his van and giving you stale buns. You say, "I noticed you pulled these from the week-old bun pile. I feel angry and cheated because I pay top dollar for fresh buns. I notice you're charging me the same as you would for fresh bread. Don't you value my business? If you give me stale buns again, I will stop buying my bread from you. I also want you to take these buns back and give me fresh buns."

You're communicating how you expect to be treated. If vendors know you will take any kind of stock they've got, they'll give you the worst and save the best for customers who have and communicate strong boundaries. That's life. You're the one who controls how others treat you by accepting how they treat you and not communicating what your expectations are.

Many people will push against your boundaries when you start using them. People who don't respect others don't like boundaries. They like to be selfish and manipulative and get what they can from others. Those who respect themselves and others will accept your boundaries. They get it. The flip side of this is learning to respect other people's boundaries. For instance, if someone tells you not to call them before 8 a.m., don't call them before 8 a.m. If their boundaries are too extreme for you, and you don't think you can meet their expectations, then you have to decide if you want to be involved with this person.

For instance, I had a massage client who insisted on taking a shower in my personal shower after her massage. I lived in a downtown loft zoned for both commercial and residential use. Most of us lived in the spaces where we worked. This not only meant I had to clean massage oil and cream out of the shower, but it often resulted in delaying my next appointment. So I expressed that boundary to her. I told her I was happy to let her use the shower for an additional fee. She insisted that the shower should be included in the cost of the massage. As a result, I ended up "firing" this client (not accepting any more appointments with her) because the inconvenience of cleaning the shower wasn't worth having the client's business. Her not being able to take a shower was something she wanted, but wasn't able to justify paying for.

Looking back I could have compromised and changed massage creams to a less oily cream, or scheduled her on a day I planned to clean the shower anyway, but even so, those weren't attractive options for me.

Boundaries are simply about honestly communicating and negotiating (or not) our needs, wants and expectations. Responsible, healthy adults can do that without yelling, criticizing, attacking or bullying others. If you're in business, you're going to meet a lot of people who think they have the right to tell you how to run your business, how you should market yourself and how you should set your prices. Without boundaries and the ability to calmly say, "Thank you for your input, I'll take it into consideration," you'll have more stress than you need.

Bill, a good friend of mine, has a small lawn care business. One day one of his customers came out into the yard drunk and, for whatever reason, starting cussing Bill for how he was doing his job. Bill smiled, held up his hand and said, "Jack, I like you. You're one of my best customers. But, I can't carry on a conversation with someone who is being verbally abusive, and so I'm going to go back to work now. I'm happy to talk with you tomorrow when you're sober, but this conversation is over." And he went back to work. The next day the customer called to apologize. He had received some bad news, started drinking and took out his frustration on Bill. Bill said he understood, but that he didn't want it to happen again, or he'd have to cancel his contract because he couldn't have himself or his employees being the brunt of something like that. The customer said he understood, and it never happened again. If Bill hadn't spoken up, the customer would have assumed it was okay to get drunk and yell at Bill or his employees.

The thing about boundaries is you can't say you'll do something you're unable or unwilling to do. For instance, Bill was willing to walk away from the contract, but if he hadn't been he could have said something like, "If this happens again I'll have to charge you double," or something that would be a consequence that got the client's attention, but didn't jeopardize Bill's contract. Ultimately he might have to give up the contract whether he wanted to or not if his boundaries were repeatedly violated.

People will treat you as well or as poorly as you train them to. Bill cared about this guy's work. But, he cared more about his employees and himself and how people treated them.

Sometimes enforcing your boundaries will result in the loss of a client or customer. But you have to determine what's important to you and how you want others to treat you. If you consistently and effectively express your boundaries and enforce them, over time you'll notice how much better people are treating you, and how much better your business is doing. The best source I've ever read for learning about boundaries is Dr. Henry Cloud's book, Boundaries, When to Say Yes, How to Say No. You can find it in most libraries. He also has some free videos on boundaries on YouTube.

If you're not sure if you have good boundaries or not, think about this. If you are feeling stressed when dealing with a customer or client, that's good evidence there's a lack of standards, policies or boundaries. If you feel overwhelmed, angry, frustrated or resentful, there's room for discovering where you lack a policy or boundary.

Lots of people would prefer that you weren't clear on what you wanted or needed. That gives them the opportunity to take advantage of you. When I felt frustrated at clients constantly changing the payment schedule with me, I realized I was always going along with them, not setting down standards in my contracts and not communicating the importance of my getting paid when they agreed to pay me. It wasn't their fault. They were treating me just like I trained them to. I had to back up, create policies and new contracts and enforce them. That meant charging a percentage for late payments and setting down clear dates in my contracts. It wasn't easy, and I felt guilty for standing up for what I needed and wanted, but you know what? The clients that valued me welcomed the clear guidelines and the ones who abused me went away. I was able to replace old clients with new ones who respected me and treated me like I expected to be treated.

Some work and business boundaries people set are around hours, scope of work and type of work. If you're not comfortable talking about "boundaries," then use the word my business partner, a lawyer, likes so much: "policies."

Policies are the same as boundaries in many ways. They describe how your business deals with different situations — anything from work hours to returns. Policies can be about anything you want to set boundaries around. They can be directed at employees and customers alike.

What hours will you work and not work? If you're homeless and have no money you may be willing to work 24/7. But after you reach a certain level of business you may want to revisit those hours. If you are simply poor, have a family and kids, you may want to tell customers you only answer the phone or respond to emails between the hours of 8 a.m. and 4 p.m. or whatever time is good for you.

How much will you do for a customer? There's customer service, and then there's going above and beyond. It's one thing to do extra for someone once in awhile, but when a customer begins to expect it, you need to charge for the service or set boundaries.

Know what your "I definitely won't _____ (fill in the blank)" standards are. I have a customer who goes out on site to work on cars. He's a mechanic, and this is a rural area. Many people have dogs that run free on their properties. He was once badly bitten by a dog and now has a strict policy/boundary. All dogs must be locked up or on a chain before he sets foot out of the car. If he arrives on site and the dogs are running loose, he simply turns around and leaves. You can forget once, but after the second time he refuses to come out to your place to work.

I once went for six months without a car, so I know how difficult it is to get around, particularly in a rural area, if you don't have a car. I depended on the kindness of friends and rental agencies for transportation. When I got a car, I offered to give other people rides. I knew they didn't have vehicles, so thought I was being a good neighbor and paying forward the help I'd received.

Eventually, however, these people started taking advantage of me because I hadn't set boundaries. They called at all hours of the day and night and were rude and abusive if I said I couldn't take them. After all, I had a business to run and couldn't drop everything to take someone to Wal-Mart because they were "bored."

I set a new boundary or policy. I would give people rides, but they had to call me at least 24 hours in advance and tell me how long they needed to be gone. Shopping trips could be 30 minutes to 4 hours. I didn't care. But I needed to know what they expected the trip to involve so I could make my own plans. If they found another ride they had to call me the minute they made other arrangements so I didn't sit in their driveway for 15 to 30 minutes wondering where they were.

The strangest thing happened. All these people stopped wanting rides. They were unable to comply with those few rules I had in place to protect me. They didn't respect me. They tried calling me 15 minutes before they wanted a ride, not the day before. I said "no," even if it was convenient. I had a boundary, and I wanted them to see I wouldn't budge from it.

Now I finally got it. It was painful. They didn't like me or appreciate me. They had used me. And I had let them. I thought I had been liked, but I had only been used and I had let it happen by not setting boundaries in the first place. If you want to be liked or respected, you must have boundaries. There are a lot of takers and users in the world, and they will use you up and throw you away if you don't have and enforce your boundaries.

CHAPTER EIGHT

Homeless Hacks — How to Find and Utilize Resources, Networking and Agency Help to Start Your Business

"If you want to go somewhere, it is best to find someone who has already been there." ~ *Robert Kiyosaki*

Whether you're homeless or not, your greatest challenge when starting a business is finding the resources and people in your area that can help you with the proper forms and paperwork to start your business. You may opt not to go formal, especially if you just plan to see if a business is right for you, or if you're just setting up shop for a week or so. There may be a particular event, such as a sports event or fair, a carnival, etc., where you find some service or product you can sell, and you don't need permits or are willing to risk not having them.

I know one woman who bought a few dozen cases of battery-powered, flickering tea light candles and sold them for $1 each at an outdoor music festival. The same candles were two for a dollar at a nearby Dollar Tree, so I'm guessing her profit on them was at least 50 cents. Judging by the number of flickering lights I saw across the lawn that night, she made over $100 for a couple of hours work. I bought five myself for my van, so I'm sure she went through all she had rather quickly. That's another reason for savings and having money in the bank. When you see an opportunity, you can seize it.

Whether you plan to follow all the laws and get licensed, or not, you still need to know the laws and the consequences so you can make an informed decision about whether or not to get a permit or license. Sometimes all you risk is a fine, other localities may decide to throw you in jail for a while. It all depends on how the municipality feels about what your business is and who you are.

No matter where you are, start by going to the local clerk's office to find out about permits and business licenses. You can find out exactly which office you need by calling information at the courthouse in the city where you are, or Googling their website and checking there. You can often find out everything you need to know about starting a business in a city or county by going to the county website.

Whether or not you know what permits or paperwork you need, make an appointment with the local SCORE office. SCORE is a nonprofit association dedicated to helping small businesses get off the ground, and grow and achieve their goals through education and mentorship. They have been doing this for more than fifty years, and the majority of SCORE programs I've seen are very good. Their website is www.score.org.

The U.S. Small Business Administration (SBA), supports their efforts, and their network of 11,000+ volunteers means you get access to mentors and people who can help you get started for low to no cost. The main SCORE headquarters told me since they are a non-profit all their services are free, but I've seen other SCORE offices that charge minimum prices for some workshops. SCORE does provide free templates, counseling, tools and workshops for anyone who wants to know more about starting a business. If there's not a SCORE office in your area, you can also get help from them online and over the telephone. If you're thinking, "Yeah, yeah, this all *sounds* good, but you want proof it can work, consider these folks:

Business: Conversation Tees
Owners: Rob Frohlking and Tom Richardson
Website: http://conversationtees.com

Rob Frohlking and Tom Richardson, both homeless, started Conversation Tees in 2015. Both currently (November 2015) live in a shelter in Raleigh, NC. Tom has an office job; Rob works for a screen printer. They started their business with very little money, drawing inspiration and resources from their current situation and a chance conversation.

The two men were staying in a homeless shelter in Raleigh, NC when they noticed a man wearing a T-shirt imprinted with one word: College. They started a conversation with the man based on the word, then realized how one word can start so many conversations, something so many people living without homes miss most. Rob's personal experience convinced him they were onto a great business idea. Rob was sleeping outside a church and a man cared enough to start a conversation. The man, a fellow musician named Stefan Youngblood, talked to Rob with respect, and engaged him in conversation. That initial conversation—followed by others, Rob said, renewed his faith. They got on the Internet at the Edenton Street Church, and started researching how to start a business. Stefan, who is also a teacher, missionary, and worship leader helped them, mentoring them and giving them feedback on the shirts. To date they've sold more than 100 shirts. Their goal is to donate a portion of all sales to the Partnership to End and Prevent Homelessness, and hopefully make enough money to set up a day center.

Business: Painters Unlimited LLC
Owner: Shaun A. Jones
Website: http://paintersunlimitedllc.com

Shaun A. Jones is a Navy veteran, a student, a body-builder and a businessman. When he was honorably discharged from the Navy he started school, studying engineering, but quickly decided the costs were prohibitive. He didn't want to graduate from college owing thousands of dollars. So he decided to start a business. After years of painting bulkheads on Navy ships his strongest skill set was painting. Thus, Painters Unlimited was born.

Shaun moved into his car, got a membership at a 24-hour gym where he could not only continue to work out, but to shower and shave every day.

He began advertising his services on FaceBook, and getting word of mouth referrals. As business picked up, he secured several large contracts and moved into an apartment. His plan is to continue to expand his business. He recently hired another painter and expects to return to school, keeping the business as a supplemental form of income after he starts his engineering career in three-five-years.

Business: The Learning Shelter
Owner: Marc Roth
Website: http://thelearningshelter.org

Marc Roth, a 16-year tech industry veteran, moved to San Francisco to take a $125,000 a year job. The job fell through, leaving him homeless and living in a shelter for the next six months. He found a flier at the shelter for TechShop, a community workshop where members can use tools and equipment, take classes and use industrial equipment to build their own projects. He used $49 of his monthly assistance stipend of $59 to buy a one month membership, and started looking for work and sending out resumes while tinkering with the equipment at the shop. Other members hired him to help them with their projects, and later TechShop hired him as a teacher. He was able to rent an apartment, move his family out to San Francisco, and launch his own business — SanFrancisco Laser.

San Francisco Laser specializes in laser cutting and etching in a variety of materials. That could have been enough, but Marc's experience awakened him to the problem of other professionals who were encountering the same thing, being homeless with no resources. San Francisco Mayor Ed Lee even mentioned Roth in his state of the city speech in 2014. The mayor said, "We're investing in people like Marc Roth. Two years ago, Marc was homeless, sleeping in shelters. He had some programming experience, but not enough to land a job. So he plunked down the last of his money to take a few advanced classes at TechShop, and then started his own business called SFLaser."

Mayor Lee later invited Roth to join him at a conference in Washington DC to speak to a group of city mayors on homelessness issues.

In 2014, he founded The Learning Shelter. The program is still in its pilot stage, but once it's funded the program will offer three months of intensive, hands-on training in printing, hardware, laser-cutting, silk-screening and other trade work with a focus on job placement at the end.

Business: Inspired Design
Owner: JL Faverio a.k.a. "Mooch"
Website: https://about.me/mooch and http://
bayareawebsitedesigner.com/

I met JL online in 2010, shortly after my TED Global talk in 2009. He was living in Los Angeles, and offering his web design services for $20 an hour. He was living out of his car by choice and putting his money into his graphics business. He founded his business, an international website and branding company, Inspired Design & Development, while homeless. He also became Unit Production Manager of a Best American Short Film Nominee, Shattered Allegiance.

Mooch is now in an apartment, but he is still inspiring people homeless or not, and telling them that anything is possible.

There are hundreds of other homeless entrepreneurs. There's Chris Gardner, who went from sleeping in public bathrooms with his toddler son, to becoming a successful stock brocker, author and motivational speaker. The movie "The Pursuit of Happyness" is based on Gardner's story. Will Smith plays Gardner in the movie.

For a short list of other homeless entrepreneurs, go to the homeless entrepreneur's club: http://theheclub.com/featured.php.

BUSINESS RESOURCES

Name: WIBO (Workshop in Business Opportunities
Phone: (212) 684-0854
Website: http://www.wibo.org
Address: 22 Cortlandt Street, 16th Floor, New York, NY
10007

Founded in 1966 in Harlem, the Workshop in Business Opportunities (WIBO) is a private non-profit organization that is committed to assisting men and women with the drive to become successful entrepreneurs. WIBO's mission is to enable small business owners and budding entrepreneurs from underserved communities to obtain financial success by starting, operating, and building successful businesses that develop economic power, provide jobs and improve communities.

WIBO's Impact: Since 1966, WIBO has developed nearly 18,000 entrepreneurs resulting in the creation of 35,000 jobs. Over 54% of WIBO graduates are in business after 5 years, compared to the national average of 20%.

Although WIBO was founded and offers workshops in:

- Harlem
- Downtown Brooklyn
- Lower East Side

- Washington Heights
- Central Brooklyn
- Financial District
- Long Island City
- South Bronx

They also work with affiliate workshops across the country:

**Name: WIBO AFFILIATE: CIC — Community Investment
Collaborative
Phone: (434) 218-3481
Website: http://www.Cicville.org
Address: PO Box 2976, Charlottesville, VA 22902
Email: Keir@Cicville.org**

The Community Investment Collaborative (CIC) is a microenterprise development organization serving the Greater Charlottesville, Virginia area providing opportunities to entrepreneurs who may lack the social, economic, or education wherewithal to establish a new business, but who have the motivation and creative drive to pursue success.

Upon graduation from the WIBO 16-week workshop, we offer entrepreneurs staged microloans up to $35,000. These loans have flexible arrangements, and we will work with you despite weak credit or collateral. Borrowers are each paired with mentors, experienced business owners who will offer you ongoing guidance and support. Throughout it all, our goal is create a comprehensive support system for local businesses.

Name: WIBO AFFILIATE: Lifebridge Community Services
Phone: (202) 368-5529
Website: http://www.LifeBrigeCT.org
Address: 475 Clinton Avenue, Bridgeport, CT 06605
Email: scarmichael@LifeBridgeCT.org

Since 1999, LifeBridge, a 501(c)(3) non-profit organization, has offered a signature Workshop in Business Opportunities (WIBO) program. LifeBridge is an affiliate of the WIBO program. The program provides 16 weeks of comprehensive business knowledge and training on all aspects of owning and running a small business. Since its inception, more than 600 participants have completed the program.

WIBO is offered twice a year in the Winter/Spring and Fall on Tuesday evenings from 6 p.m. to 9 p.m. Go to their website to fill out an online application and to get more information. LifeBridge understands that people impacted by poverty are challenged by a range of complex social, economic, and health issues, and that their plight affects the quality of life and stability of our communities. Each client in the LifeBridge program receives an individual plan of comprehensive services that are delivered through their four core programs: Economic Empowerment, Youth Services, Behavioral Health, and Social Enterprises.

In addition to the WIBO program, the Small Business Development program offers monthly workshops on a variety of topics to help small business owners grow and succeed. The workshops are open to the general public and upcoming events can be viewed on the Economic Empowerment calendar on the LifeBridge website.

Name: WIBO AFFILIATE: AltCap Formerly known as CKMOCDE
Phone: (816) 216-1851
Website: http://www.kcmocde.org
Address: Kansas City, Missouri
Email: christine_kahm@kcmocde.org

AltCap is a community development financial institution (CDFI) committed to serving as a catalyst for investment in economically distressed communities throughout Kansas City, Missouri.

As a mission-based, 501(c)(4) CDFI, AltCap provides alternative capital through a wide range of financial products and programs that are meant to support critical investments in economically distressed communities not adequately served by traditional financial institutions.

Name: WIBO AFFILIATE: RVAWORKS
Phone: (804) 421-4002
Website: http://www.richmondeda.org/
Address: 501 East Franklin Street, Richmond, VA 23219
Email: dale.fickett@richmoneda.org

RVA Works (formerly Advantech) will host a new program to encourage business ownership, job creation, and economic growth for Richmond and the region. Entrepreneur Institute is an 18 week program to provide prospective business owners required skills, mentorship, local professional connections, and access to finance.

RVA Works goal is to contribute directly to diverse economic growth and job creation by fostering entrepreneurship and innovation. Inclusive programs the program offers creates new livelihoods in under-resourced communities, and supporting higher-growth innovators through:

- Outreach to under-resourced communities
- Solidarity in our startup community
- Facilities for entrepreneurs
- Acceleration of new social innovators (coming soon)

Name: WIBO AFFILIATE: Grace Hill

Phone: (314) 584-6841

Website: http://gracehillsettlement.org

Address: Grace Hill Settlement House, 2600 Hadley Street,

Saint Louis, MO 63106

Email: alwilson@gracehillsettlement.org

Grace Hill is comprised of sister agencies, Grace Hill Health Centers, Inc. (GHHC) and Grace Hill Settlement House (GHSH). Each is controlled by a separate governing body. Grace Hill Settlement House was founded in 1903 by the Episcopal Diocese to help immigrant families "settle into their new neighborhood" on the near north side of St. Louis. Now it serves neighborhoods throughout the City of St. Louis and St. Charles County with its MORE system.

Grace Hill Health Centers began in 1906 with a small community health and pharmaceutical service. Now it operates five Health Centers and a community health program in the city. Today, Grace Hill serves neighborhoods throughout the St. Louis region with a combined population in excess of 100,000 people.

Name: Woodforest National Bank

Phone: 1-877-968-7962 Toll-free

Website: https://woodforest.com

Woodforest National Bank is the only bank I'm listing because (1) I bank with them and have experience with their service and services. (2) They are located in most 24-hour Wal-Mart stores and so are located around the country. (3) They are open seven days a week, yes, even on Sundays in some locations and (4) they help the small businessman/woman and they are truly community oriented. Go to their website for more details and information, but here are the basics from their website:

They are committed to the provision of affordable housing and homeownership opportunities. Through their community partners and community outreach efforts, Woodforest provided over $73 million in affordable housing and homeownership financing for families in their communities in 2012 - 2015.

Woodforest demonstrates a commitment to affordable housing and homeownership through community partnerships with community based organizations, including Habitat for Humanity, as well as local community based organizations, government organizations, and affordable housing providers.

Habitat for Humanity:

Woodforest seeks opportunities to meet the needs of affordable housing in communities. From 2013 through September of 2015, Woodforest National Bank collaborated with 23 Habitat for Humanity affiliates providing $209,600 in investment grants.

Patricia Brown, Sr. Vice President of Woodforest National Bank and Board Member of Habitat for Humanity Montgomery County Texas stated,

"We are proud to partner with Habitat for Humanity and to realize, first hand, what can be accomplished when we all work together. It was so rewarding to work alongside the homeowners and to witness the pride they took in building their very own home from the ground up."

Woodforest also offers a basic, easy to understand, three class course on managing your finances called Banking GPS. I've been impressed with the branch I work with, and the customer service representatives I've encountered. I like them because the small business owner can upload money to their debit card, do both personal and business banking and get assistance with their financial questions. I'm sure other banks do the same, but Woodforest has been the one bank I've seen deliver for me.

Places that help the homeless nationally and regionally:

National Alliance to End Homelessness
Phone: 202-638-1526
Website: http://www.endhomelessness.org
Address: 1518 K Street NW, 2nd Floor,
Washington, DC 20005
Email: info@naeh.org

Although primarily a research, policy, education and opinion center, (they don't hand out food, clothing, shelter, etc.) this is a good site to visit to learn more about homelessness in general, or to find out about new trends.

National Coalition for Homeless Veterans
Phone: Veteran in crisis? Call 1-877-424-3838 for
assistance 24/7
Website: http://nchv.org

The National Coalition for Homeless Veterans (NCHV) is a 501(c)(3) nonprofit organization governed by a 23-member board of directors. The NCHV is the resource and technical assistance center for a national network of community-based service providers and local, state and federal agencies that provide emergency and supportive housing, food, health services, job training and placement assistance, legal aid and case management support for homeless veterans.

NCHV also serves as the primary liaison between the nation's care providers, Congress and the executive branch agencies charged with helping them succeed in their work. NCHV's advocacy has strengthened and increased funding for virtually every federal homeless veteran assistance program in existence today.

Under a technical assistance grant awarded by the Department of Labor-Veterans' Employment and Training Service, NCHV provides guidance and information about program development, administration, governance and funding to all of the nation's homeless veteran service providers.

In November 2015, the U.S. Department of Housing and Urban Development (HUD) and the U.S. Department of Veterans Affairs (VA) announced nearly $12 million to 79 local public housing agencies across the country to provide a permanent home to veterans experiencing homelessness. The supportive housing assistance is provided through the HUD-Veterans Affairs Supportive Housing (HUD-VASH) program which combines rental assistance from HUD with case management and clinical services provided by VA.

According to press releases, HUD is providing $6.4 million to 27 local Public Housing Agencies (PHAs) to provide permanent supportive housing to an estimated 821 veterans. These vouchers are being awarded through the

HUD-VASH Project-based Voucher Set-Aside competition, announced in June 2015. These PBVS will enable homeless veterans and their families to access affordable housing with an array of supportive services.

HUD is also providing 52 PHAs with a total of $5.4 million Extraordinary Administrative Fees (EAF) to support their HUD-VASH programs and reduce the amount of time that it takes for a veteran to locate and move into permanent housing

HomeAid Northern Virginia
Phone: 571-283-6300 and for Women Giving Back 703-554-9386
Website: http://www.homeaidnova.org/in-our-community/resources/
Address: 3684 Centerview Drive, Suite 110B, Chantilly, Virginia 20151
Email: info@HomeAidNoVa.org

HomeAid Northern Virginia is a small non-profit organization that leverages the resources of the homebuilding community and its corporate partners to conduct major renovations to facilities that house the homeless. Please note that they do not assist individuals or families with finding housing. They work directly with shelter organizations to build or renovate housing facilities. If you need assistance in finding housing, please check their resources page (shown above) for links to organizations that may be able to help. Shelter projects help families and individuals gain stability and a place to thrive.

HomeAid works with partner homebuilders and others to provide much-needed project management and building services to homeless services providers across Northern Virginia. Due to their partnerships, they are able to significantly reduce the cost of constructions to service provider organizations. This allows them to redirect those dollars back into programs and services for homeless families and individuals, such as financial education, job skills training and other programs that enable people take steps towards self-sufficiency and a better life.

HomeAid also works with the homeless, and with women and children. HomeAid's *Women Giving Back* (WGB) program provides a basic necessity — clothing. Women and children referred by area service provider organizations can shop at The WGB Store free-of-charge for professional clothing — clothing that will allow them to participate fully in the workplace and give them the boost of self-confidence they need to make a new start.

The Salvation Army
Phone: Go the Salvation Army website and enter your zip code for a local phone number
Website: http://salvationarmyusa.org
Address: National Headquarters, 615 Slaters Lane, P.O. Box 269, Alexandria, VA 22313

Email: Go the Salvation Army website and enter your zip code for a local email address

The Salvation Army is an international movement. It is an evangelical part of the universal Christian Church with a message based on the Bible. Its ministry is motivated by the love of God. Its mission is to preach the gospel of Jesus Christ and to meet human needs in His name without discrimination. Although they are a Christian organization, the Salvation Army serves nearly 30 million Americans — or one person every second — from a variety of backgrounds. People who come to the organization for assistance will be served according to their need and the Salvation Army's capacity to help — regardless of race, gender, ethnicity or sexual orientation.

They can help with:
- Emergency assistance
- Rehabilitation
- Worship services
- Youth services
- Family counseling
- Mailing list preferences

Other services in your community

GOODWILL Industries
Phone: For immediate help finding a job call 800-Goodwill (800-466-3945)
Website: http://www.goodwill.org
Address: 15810 Indianola Drive, Rockville, MD 20855
Email: contactus@goodwill.org

Goodwill's focus is on jobs. Their AbilityOne program is the largest provider of employment opportunities for those who are either blind or have significant disabilities. They employ approximately 46,000 people through more than 600 nonprofit agencies, including Goodwill. Goodwill Industries provides a broad range of commercial business services to government agencies, such as custodial work, food service, landscaping, manufacturing, and document management.

They also provide Temporary Assistance to Needy Families (TANF). The TANF program was created in 1996, replacing the Aid to Families with Dependent Children Program, which provided cash assistance to poor families since 1935. Since TANF was created, Goodwils have provided services to more than 1.5 million TANF recipients.

According to Goodwill's website, they are the nation's leading provider of job-training services, with a long history (dating back to World War I) of helping returning veterans — many with disabilities and other employment challenges — reenter the workforce and society.

They also help those with criminal backgrounds. As the nation's largest provider of job-training services, they call upon key stakeholders, including state and federal policymakers, judges, law enforcement officials, service providers (including local Goodwill agencies), educators, employers, and victims, to come together to create systemic changes that hold offenders accountable, minimize the negative effects on their communities and families, and support people with criminal backgrounds who want to re-enter society and make a positive contribution.

Goodwill's Senior Community Service Employment Program (SCESP) helps provide low-income older workers with community service employment and private sector job placements. As a national SCSEP grantee, they support policies and federal investments that help older workers participate in the workforce and reauthorization of the Older Americans Act (OAA).

As North America's leading nonprofit provider of employment training, Goodwill also helps with job placement services and other community programs for people looking to secure employment and build their skills. They say they advocate for training and employment opportunities that help a variety of populations find jobs and careers. Why not stop into your local Goodwill and see if they have counselors who can help you on your way to starting and running your business!

The National Coalition for the Homeless
Phone: 202-462-4822
Website: http://nationalhomeless.org
Address: 2201 P St NW, Washington, DC 20037
Email: info@nationalhomeless.org

The National Coalition for the Homeless is a national network of people who are currently experiencing or who have experienced homelessness. They work with activists and advocates, community-based and faith-based service providers, and others committed to a single mission: To prevent and end homelessness while ensuring the immediate needs of those experiencing homelessness are met and their civil rights protected.

The NCH envisions a world where everyone has a safe, decent, affordable and accessible home. According to their website, they are committed to creating the systemic and attitudinal changes necessary to prevent and end homelessness.

Their first principle of practice is that people who are currently experiencing homelessness or have formerly experienced homelessness must be actively involved in all of their work. Their programs are centered around public education, policy advocacy, and grassroots organizing, and are focused on the issues of housing justice, economic justice, health care justice, and civil rights. They also have a pretty good directory of resources all over the country. There is no centralized list of resources, but here is the link to their directory: http://nationalhomeless.org/references/directory/

Homeless is Not My Choice
Phone: 520-603-9932
Website: http://homelessisnotmychoice.org
Address: 2201 P St NW, Washington, DC 20037
Email: info@homelessisnotmychoice.org

Homeless Is Not My Choice is a nonprofit organization dedicated to uplifting those individuals who are homeless, or near homeless, because of foreclosures, economic recession, an uncaring and insensitive government, or corporate greed. They, as their website puts it, "Help those who want to be helped." They not only feed the homeless (in exchange for six hours of work for three meals a day), but they house and train those willing to learn a vocation.

To find the most comprehensive list for your city/state, visit any shelter or organization near you and ask for a list of available resources. Every community and/or shelter will have the names, phone numbers and addresses of local shelters, food kitchens, programs and resources. If you don't know where to find a shelter, or can't access a computer, call the local police department, or a local church or synagogue.

CHAPTER NINE

How and Where to Find Resources in Your State
If You're Homeless, Poor, Broke or Hungry

"Every accomplishment starts with the decision to try."

All this talk about starting a business is fine, but it's hard to think about business or anything else if you're hungry, wet and cold. If you haven't had any sleep in a long, long time you're not going to be able to focus on a business. The one thing that makes a difference is not what you have, or don't have. The one thing that makes a difference is your decision to try, to fail and to get up and try again. The resources, the opportunities, the people, networks, mentors and customers are out there, but *you* have to be the one who decides to go after them.

There are dozens of organizations that help the homeless. **The Homeless Shelter Directory** is a great place to start, but you'll need Internet access.

http://www.homelessshelterdirectory.org/

They have information about soup kitchens, resources, and shelter, rent assistance programs, affordable housing and all kinds of information for all 50 states. The Homeless Shelter Directory includes all resources necessary to help the needy.

The directory was also created for people who want to find and donate food and/or supplies to their local shelter. Volunteer opportunities are also available at most shelters. The directory's owner has listed contact information for volunteering at these shelters. Many shelters have waiting lists, so it's best to call before going to the shelter. If you can't or don't find what you need on the directory, do a local search. Many new shelters or programs may not have made it to the national list.

The best place to start finding local resources is to go to your local library and Google "Homeless and _____," the name of the state and city where you are. There are, for instance, 17 shelters in Charlottesville, Virginia, listed at http://www.suntopia.org/charlottesville/va/ homeless_shelters.php. Charlottesville also has PACEMShelter.org during the winter months.

There are food banks, food pantries and soup kitchens. Charlottesville has pretty much become a homeless destination because of the level of services provided. They also have the Community Investment Collaborative (CIC). CIC is an 18-week program that teaches students of all ages how to start a business. More information is available at its website, http://cicville.org.

There is a cost, but there are scholarships, and I'm also interested in starting a program for homeless entrepreneurs. Stay tuned to my website, *thehomelessentrepreneur.com* for more information and details about that, as well as information about business and entrepreneurship in general.

If you are in a rural area, you may not find as many resources as you would in a city. You may need certain services, but may be unwilling to leave a city where you know where everything is. Consider looking for other areas where you can find the resources you need, the employment you seek or the business mentoring you want to pursue. You can always move back later when you're back on your feet.

Starting a business isn't for everybody. It's not a stop-gap solution for making money fast. While you may have a good day, or a good season selling something, that's not typical. If you absolutely, positively must make money quickly, you may get lucky like James did — and hit on the perfect business plan that can be executed the same day and result in the sales you want and need to get what you want and need.

There are essential services almost every city has, and then there are services unique to certain areas. The Homeless Garden Project in Santa Cruz, California, for instance, provides job training, transitional employment and support services to people who are homeless. They work with volunteers and the homeless, and blend formal, hands-on and service-learning on their 3-acre organic farm and among their related enterprises.

Other homeless garden projects raise food to feed the homeless.

HomelessIsNotMyChoice. Homeless Is Not My Choice is a nonprofit organization dedicated to uplifting those individuals who are homeless, or near homeless, because of foreclosures, economic recession, an uncaring and insensitive government, or corporate greed. They, as their website puts it, "Help those who want to be helped." They not only feed the homeless (in exchange for six hours of work for three meals a day), but they house and train those willing to learn a vocation.

If you're newly homeless, homeless for the first time, or are about to become homeless, you may or may not be familiar with the basic services available to you. If you have lost your utilities, talk to your utility company representative.

There are programs designed to restore your services and pay your bills for you. People who lose essential services like water, electric and gas are more likely to become homeless. If you can find a way to keep the power on by talking to different programs and agencies, do so. Don't wait until you're homeless to start looking for help. If you're hurting financially, start looking now for help. Start asking everyone you meet, whether it's a clerk, or someone who takes your payment at the utility company, your landlord, a neighbor — anyone. Just ask if they know where to find help, or if they know someone who might know where you could learn more or get help. Ask. No one is going to volunteer the information unless they know you want it.

A business is a great way to find that extra income. It doesn't have to be a super big business either. All you need is something you can make, do, fix or create that others are willing to pay for.

You may choose not to use these services, but to find a way to survive without them. I wish I had known about these places and taken advantage of them more often. I was working, but my money went to keep the van working so I could keep a job and pay for a storage unit, so I had a place to sleep during the day and to store my stuff. It's not something I would advocate now, but I did the best I could with what I had.

You may choose to do the same, live in your car and buy food, or cook out of your car. I suggest saving your money for a vehicle, or other purposes, and using the systems communities have put into place to help those who need help. Most people are only homeless 30 to 90 days while they find a new job, affordable housing or family members and friends who can/will help them. In the meantime, don't be ashamed to apply for food stamps or other social services — especially if you have children. Local food stamp offices are listed in the state or local government pages of the telephone book. The office should be listed under "Food Stamps," "Social Services," "Human Services," "Public Assistance" or a similar title. You can also call your state's SNAP hotline number. Most are toll-free numbers.

SOUP KITCHENS

Soup kitchens are places that serve the poor, homeless, destitute and hungry. They can be found in churches, homes, parks, homeless shelters or anyplace where volunteers and organizations exist to serve the homeless. Some are large; some are small. Some are merely volunteers handing out bagged lunches. Many soup kitchens are found in churches. Some operate out of food trucks or the trunk of a car. Their goal is to feed the hungry and poor. Some are located in the basements of churches or community centers. In many communities the location of the soup kitchen varies with the day of the week. Check around. You don't have to go hungry.

SHELTERS

Homeless shelters run the gamut of the good, the bad, the ugly and the safe or unsafe. Remember, most shelters house the chronically homeless, many of whom are mentally ill, addicts or child molesters who can't find housing because of their criminal record. Your experience will vary according to the shelter, the volunteers, the population, the size of the city, the demand on the shelter and whether you are female, male or have a family/children with you. During times of extreme cold, you're safer and better off in a shelter if you can find one with an available bed.

FOOD BANKS

Food banks, or food pantries as they're often called, are non-profit hunger relief organizations that receive food donations from companies and communities and churches to distribute to the disadvantaged, homeless or poor. Food banks are found in most communities and rely on donors and volunteers to carry out day-to-day operations. A food bank's sole purpose is to help the hungry.

There is no one source for all things helpful for the homeless person or family. Ultimately it's up to you to make the choices that best fit your circumstances. Being homeless is a number-one fear for many because it's the closest many of us will come to feeling like we're going to die.

If you have a family member or friend who is homeless, you may be reading this book hoping to find an answer for them. I wish it were that easy. Getting off of the streets, even with family and friends helping, is very hard. Without friends or family, it's even more difficult. I was fortunate to have a brother who sent me gas money, and friends who offered me their spare beds or a spot in their driveways.

I was fortunate enough to have a van that ran long enough for me to live in it while I was homeless. The repairs were simple enough that I could also learn to do them myself. God blessed me, bringing people and circumstances into my life that got me to where I am. But I too am still only a few paychecks or a severe medical crisis away from homelessness. We all are. The illusion that security is something you can guarantee is smoke and mirrors. Just ask any of the millionaires defrauded by Bernie Madoff now forced to live like the other 99 percent of America.

A medical crisis, an accident at work, a divorce, disability or a death can and do affect millions of people every day. Businesses and companies fail, and layoffs devastate millions. The only security you have when it comes to employment is owning your own company. At least you know you're in control and making the decisions you think are best.

Sound financial planning, saving, learning to create a passive income online (topic for another book), are all ways you can ensure you don't end up back on the street. I hope this book inspired you to take control of your life and do something for yourself. If you're willing to work hard, you deserve more than minimum wage, and you can have it if you start your own business. Being a business owner isn't a magic bullet. You'll trade one kind of stress for another, but you'll be the one in control, making the decisions. There won't be anyone else to blame. If you start a business and succeed, however, your entire world can change for the better.

Most homeless people I've met are single, but there are millions of homeless families, or single parents with children. Even if you're not homeless, but you can "see it" from where you are, starting a business is still a great option. You'll find you're able to stay home with your children, or be able to be with your children during the day if you're on the street. Having your own business ensures you don't have to put your child in daycare. I know families whose children help with their business, whether it's putting labels on products, mixing the ingredients for soap, or cleaning up around the workspace. People with families find they can work fewer hours, but make more money, leaving them time to cope with health issues, or travel, or do more of what they want if they start their own business. Remember, this book is to show you that anyone can start and succeed in business, even if you're homeless, but also if you're poor or broke.

If you take nothing else away from this book, I hope you'll remember that homeless, broke or poor is NOT who you are, it's only where you are right now. And you have the power to change that.

EPILOGUE

Even before this book was published a great many people expressed interest in using it to create classes to help those people in homeless shelters, church programs and even one-on-one with "how-to-start" a business. As a result of the input, suggestions and requests I have received I started a workbook to accompany this book. It will be out sometime in Februrary, so please check CreateSpace or Amazon.com for it. The name will be: *The Homeless Entrepreneur Workbook*.

For more information, articles, inspiration and news you may also visit http://thehomelessentrepreneur.com.